THE STONES CRY OUT

The Stones Cry Out

God's Best Kept Secrets
Hidden in Stone

BY
BONNIE GAUNT

Bonnie Gaunt, 510 Golf Avenue, Jackson, Michigan 49203, U.S.A.

Library of Congress Catalog Card Number: 91-92021

ISBN: 0-9602688-2-0

PUBLISHED BY

HOFFMAN PRINTING CO.
P.O. Box 1529
Muskogee, Oklahoma 74402
(918) 682-8341
www.artisanpublishers.com

ISBN 0-9602688-2-0
COPYRIGHT © 1991
ALL RIGHTS RESERVED

Dedicated to my husband
Ralph
for his encouragement,
love and patience
during the many hours of study
in the preparation
of this book.

FOREWORD

There is a remarkable correlation of numbers that exists in the universe. These numbers reveal a divine thread of evidence regarding the story of creation, the story of man, and of man's destiny. The ancient Pythagoras discovered that all creation can be reduced to simple numbers; however, in recent years, it has been found that those numbers not only reveal a logical pattern, but they also reveal the Creator.

In this work it has been my purpose to attempt to pull back the curtain ever so slightly, and search for a small glimpse of the intelligence that patterned the universe. It was rewarding indeed to find that the Creator has left his footprints, hidden in number, hidden in stone.

It was the belief of Pythagoras that the building blocks of creation were to be found in numbers. In the ages since, those building blocks have been defined and charted in the periodic table of the elements, which reduces them to simple numbers. It was exciting to find a relationship between the numbers of creation, and the numbers of the Creator.

It is my joy and my hope that this study will touch your heart as it has touched mine.

Bonnie Gaunt, 1991

Contents

The Great Pyramid—the jewel in the desert.

Stonehenge no longer bares its ancient stones to the hands and feet of tourists.

The Great Pyramid keeps its lonely, timeless vigil over the Nile delta.

1

"The Stones Cry Out"

It's a strange phrase—"The stones will cry out"—but those remarkable words were spoken by one who left his indelible signature on the pages of time.

The scene was a warm spring day on a country road that descended from the Mount of Olives, through the Kidron Valley and up the steep hill to Jerusalem. A little band of men were making their way up the winding road. Excitement was in the air! The long-promised kingdom—the kingdom of which the ancient prophets had spoken—seemed almost within reach; and the one whom they were proclaiming as the new king was in their midst, riding on a young colt.

As they neared Jerusalem the people along the way became caught up in the excitement. They began laying their garments on the path to give him a royal welcome. And in their exuberance they began shouting *"Hosanna to the Son of David: blessed is he that cometh in the name of the Lord."*

There were some in the crowd who rebuked them for their shouting. Then Jesus, who sat on the colt, exclaimed, *"If these should hold their peace, the stones would immediately cry out."*

It was not an incidental choice of words.

Stones have been the mouthpiece through which God has spoken to man; the instrument through which he has concealed and revealed His plan of the ages. A plan that touches the lives of every one of us.

Throughout His written word, no less than 55 times, He calls himself the Rock. This same symbol of power, strength, endurance, and everlastingness is similarly given to Jesus Christ more than 25 times.

The symbol is telling us something magnificent! The search for the understanding of it is a glorious quest, for it gives us an insight into the mind of the Creator, and into the laws that form the very foundation of the universe.

The Foundation of the Earth

The search for the basic building blocks of the universe is nearly as old as man. In the 5th century B.C. the Greek philosopher and mathematician, Pythagoras, probed the wonders of nature and left for us a legacy that has been subsequently revered by all the ages of man. He taught that nature is commanded by numbers. There is a harmony in nature, he said, a unity in its variety, and it speaks to us in a language: numbers are the language of nature. He was a pioneer in linking geometry with numbers, not only in the material world, but also with sound, light and vision. He felt that the agreement between nature and number was so cogent that not only the sounds of nature, but all her characteristic dimensions were simple numbers that express harmonies. Pythagoras had discovered a profound truth!

In the year A.D. 1905, a young physicist named Albert Einstein rocked the world of science and physics with his now famous paper, *The Electrodynamics of Moving Bodies,* in which he linked light to time, time to space, energy to matter, matter to space, and space to gravitation. In short, he drew the universe together in a simple formula: $E = mc^2$ — energy equals mass times the speed of light squared.

What this really means is that energy and mass are interconvertible. That being true, we can turn the equation around and state it as $m = E \div c^2$, or mass equals energy divided by the speed of light squared. The implications are startling! Could Einstein have indeed discovered the formula for creation?

Before proceeding with this analogy it is necessary to acquaint the reader with some of the fundamentals of gematria. The Old Testament was originally written in the Hebrew language, and the New Testament in Greek. These two languages are unique in that their alphabets also served as a numbering system. Each letter of the Hebrew and Greek alphabet had a number equivalent. Thus every word, phrase, name and place in the Bible has a number equivalent. (An in-depth description of gematria and how it works is given in Appendix I, which please see.)

A study of the numbers given in scripture reveals that the basic foundation number of all creation is 12. However, the word *creation* in Greek, $\kappa\tau\iota\sigma\iota\varsigma$, has a number equivalent of 740. The word *foundation* in the Hebrew scriptures is יסד, which has a number equivalent of 74.

In Psalm 102:25 we are told *"Thou hast laid the foundations of the earth."* That statement in the original Hebrew was הארין יסדת and had a number equivalent of 740.

A most remarkable fact emerges when we take those two foundation numbers and multiply them:

$$12 \times 74 = 888$$

The name Jesus in New Testament Greek is Ἰησους, and bears the number equivalent of 888. The equation is, in fact, saying "The foundation of creation is Jesus." This was testified by the Apostle John: *"All things were made by him, and without him was not anything made that was made,"* (John 1:3). And again in verse 10 *"The world was made by him."*

Change the equation: substitute plus for times and it would look like this:

$$12 + 74 = 86$$

The name God in Hebrew is אלהים, and bears the number 86. These two foundation numbers are telling us *"In the beginning God created the heaven and the earth,"* (Genesis 1:1). But how! What were the building blocks?

The profound truth that Einstein discovered and gave to the world in 1905 gives us a glimpse into the work of creation—mass is equal to energy divided by the speed of light squared. The source of all energy is the power of the Creator.

Someone once said that the only absolute in science is that there are no absolutes. If this were true it would set the scientist adrift without rudder or sail in a sea of unconnected facts. Nature itself reveals the necessity for absolutes—yet finding them may not be within the realm of man's ability.

Man's search for an absolute has brought him to the basic fundamental necessity for the existence of all matter—the speed of light.

For many centuries men thought that light acted instantaneously regardless of distance. Galileo attempted to measure the speed of light by timing flashes of light between two distant hilltops. In 1675 Olaus Roemer, a Danish astronomer, determined the speed of light to be about 186,000 miles a second by studying the eclipses of the moons encircling the planet Jupiter, from two different positions of the earth's orbit. The results he obtained were surprisingly close to those obtained with modern instruments.

In 1950 a British physicist, Louis Essen, announced a new determination for the speed of light, 186,282 miles a second, by measuring the frequency and length of radio waves. The figure was later confirmed in the United States and Sweden, however, not all scientists have accepted it.

The rounded figure of 186,000 miles per second is generally used to define the speed of light through empty space.

The interrelationship between the speed of light and matter gives cause for some interesting analogies.

Our earth revolves on its axis, making one revolution every 24 hours. Because the earth also revolves around the sun, we have daylight over that portion of the earth facing the sun. Because of the tilt of earth's axis in relation to the sun, our length of night and day varies with the seasons—indeed, it causes the seasons. However, at the equinox we enjoy equal periods of night and day; each becoming 12 hours in length (12 being the foundation number relative to the earth).

The earth, in its eliptical orbit around the sun, requires 365.242 earth days to complete the circuit. If this figure defined one side of a square, the perimeter of that square would be 1460 units.

THE STONES CRY OUT

365.242 = one side
1460 = perimeter

Redefine that perimeter of 1460 units as a circle with a circumference of 1460 units.

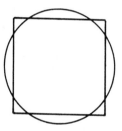

Now draw a square tangent to the circle, and the perimeter of the new square will be 1860 units.

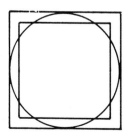

The 186 defines the speed of light. Remember the formula $m = E \div c^2$, mass equals energy divided by the speed of light squared. The source of energy must be from the Creator, for when we build the model one step further, and redefine the outer square as a circle of the same perimeter, and then draw a square tangent to that circle, the perimeter of the big square would be 2368. The name Jesus Christ, 'Ιησους Χριστος, has a number equivalent of 2368.

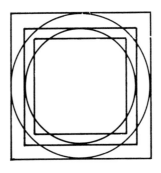

Perimeter of small square	1460
Perimeter of middle square	1860
Perimeter of large square	2368

"All things were made by Him; and without Him was not anything made that was made," (John 1:3).

The Earth's Crust

The earth is essentially a mass of rock—magma, or molten rock within, and solidified, or cooled rock without. 99% of the rock which comprises earth's crust is composed of twelve elements. Again 12, the foundation number, is an integral part of earth's structure. Below are listed these 12 elements in their order of abundance, and beside each element is its atomic number (the number of protons in its nucleus).

Oxygen	8
Silicon	14
Aluminum	13
Iron	26
Calcium	20
Sodium	11
Potassium	19
Magnesium	12
Titanium	22
Phosphorus	15
Hydrogen	1
Manganese	25
	186

The total of the atomic numbers that constitute earth's crust is 186—the number that represents the speed of light.

The Creator is spoken of in scripture as the personification of light as well as of rock. It was not by coincidence that the Psalmist wrote, *"Jehovah is my Rock,"* (Psalm 18:2), יהוה, סלע —the name bears the number equivalent of 186.

Moses wrote it in song when he said *"He is the Rock, His Work is perfect,"* (Deuteronomy 32:4). By the phrase *"His Work,"* Moses was obviously referring to the work of creation. The phrase in the original Hebrew is פעלו and bears the number 186.

The prophet Isaiah spoke of the time when God's peaceable kingdom would be established in the earth and used these descriptive words:

Behold, a king shall reign in righteousness, and princes shall rule in judgment. And a man shall be as a hiding place from the wind, and a covert from the tempest; as rivers of water in a dry place, as the shadow of a great Rock in a weary land," (Isaiah 32:1, 2).

The beauty of the word picture comes alive with meaning when we realize the number equivalent for *"great Rock,"* סלע כבד , is 186.

9

THE STONES CRY OUT

When Jesus rode into Jerusalem that memorable day in A.D. 33, with the crowds shouting *"Hosanna to the King,"* he did not rebuke them for their exuberance and their noise because the time had come for him to be proclaimed king. He knew that he would be the one to fulfill Isaiah's prophecy: *"A King shall reign in righteousness."* But he also knew that before his exaltation as king, he must first give his life to redeem the human family. Within a few short but eventful days, the one whom they had proclaimed king, hung dying on a cross atop Golgotha's hill.

The name Golgotha means "place of the skull." It indeed was well-named, for the caves in its sides give it the appearance of a skull. Golgotha in Greek is Γολγοθα and has the number equivalent of 186.

The Building Blocks of Creation

The search for the building blocks of creation has occupied men's minds from earliest times. To the ancient Greeks it appeared sensible to assume that there might be some kind of ultimate building blocks of matter. Many centuries later, Isaac Newton concluded that matter was formed in "solid, massy, hard, impenetrable, moving particles." Although later physicists felt that Newton was rather naive in this concept, today's quantum mechanics gives some validity to his ideas, suggesting small particles called *neutrinos* (little neutral ones). The first man to suggest the atom's existence was John Dalton, in the early 19th century.

Dalton developed the concept of the atomic weights of the elements. The weight of one atom compared with the weight of a carbon atom that was established as exactly 12 (the foundation number). In so doing, he found that when elements combine together to form new compounds, even though the element's atomic weight may be expressed in decimals, they always combine in proportions that can be expressed in whole numbers—a unique phenomenon in physical nature.

Apparently Pythagoras was right—nature is commanded by number.

Today, what is known as the periodic table of the elements

is available in any highschool science room[1]. They are arranged in family groups within the hierarchy of matter. However, one element stands out as different. It does not fit into any family group. Some have called it the "lone wolf." The element is hydrogen.

Hydrogen is unique among the elements. Its nucleus consists of one proton which is orbited by one electron. When hydrogen is placed in a tube and then charged with high-voltage electricity, its single electron will jump to a higher orbit. Subsequently it will fall back into its lower orbit, but when it does, it emits a quantum of energy which shows up as a beautiful red in the spectrum—hydrogen's characteristic color.

Hydrogen molecules consist of two atoms clinging together. At great heats the nuclei of the two atoms fuse, releasing vast amounts of energy. The sun is almost pure hydrogen. The thermonuclear fusion of its hydrogen lights and heats the universe. Hydrogen is therefore necessary to all life on earth.

Hydrogen has an atomic number of 1, and an atomic weight of 1.0080. Its density at 32^0 F is .00008. Remarkable numbers! They tell of the Creator himself—the source of light and life to all His creation.

In the book of Revelation, the Apostle John records the signature of the One who gave him the revelation:

I am Alpha and Omega, the beginning and the ending, saith the Lord, which is, and which was, and which is to come, the Almighty.

In the Greek alphabet, Alpha carries the number equivalent of 1, and Omega the number 800. These two numbers, 1 and 8, not only define the hydrogen atom, but the Creator and his plan for the redemption of men through Jesus Christ.

Share with me for a moment the joy of these number symbols.

First, the atomic number, being 1, is personified by the Creator and his work of creation and salvation. The number 1 is a fitting symbol of the One who said *"I am God, I change not."* The

---

[1] The periodic table of the elements was developed by Dmitri Mendeleyev in 1869.

number 1 always retains its integrity, it never changes; thus the square of 1 is still 1. The number 1, being indivisible, is independent of all others and it is the source of all others. Just as the creation finds its origin in the Creator. One denotes the beginning, and our Bible clearly begins with the statement, *"In the beginning God. . ."*

God declared of himself *"I am the first, I am the last, and beside me there is no God,"* (Isaiah 44:6)

1   Alpha α

10   The one exalted נבה

100 A great God is Jehovah אל גדול יהוה

100 Power פף

100 My King (Psalm 2:6) מלכי

1000 Lord $\kappa\upsilon\rho\acute{\iota}o\upsilon$

1000 Everlasting power $\mathring{\alpha}\mathring{\iota}\delta\iota os\ \delta\acute{\upsilon}\nu\alpha\mu\iota s$

110 Foundation מוסד

110 Your King (Zechariah 9:9) מלכך

1100 Unexcelling greatness (Eph. 1:19) $\mathring{\upsilon}\pi\epsilon\rho\beta\acute{\alpha}\lambda\lambda o\nu\ \mu\acute{\epsilon}\gamma\epsilon\theta os$

111 The Most High (Daniel 4:32) עליא

111 House (my Father's house—John 14:2) $o\mathring{\iota}\kappa\acute{\iota}\alpha$

111 Wonderful (Isaiah 9:6) פלא

111 Great wonder פלא

111 Nurture $\pi\alpha\iota\delta\epsilon\acute{\iota}\alpha$

111 Red ארמוני

1110 The root of Jesse (Isaiah 11:10) שׁרשׁ ישׁ

1111 My name (Revelation 2:13) $\tau\grave{o}\ \mathring{o}\nu o\mu\acute{\alpha}\ \mu o\upsilon$

1111 Name of the Son (I John 5:13) $\mathring{o}\nu o\mu\alpha\ \upsilon\mathring{\iota}o\hat{\upsilon}$

101 Michael (Daniel 12:1) מיכאל

The second number relating to the hydrogen atom is 8. All who have attempted a study of the numbers in holy scripture have agreed, 8 is the number that represents a new beginning—a number that depicts Jesus and the work of redemption.

8   Beginning אֵ

8   Save η

8   "He who comes" ("Blessed is he who comes in the name of the Lord —Psalm 118:26) הבא

80   To make perfect בָּלַל

80   Foundation יסוֹד

80   "Laid the foundation" (Zechariah 4:9) יסד

80   "Right hand" (Right hand of God—Romans 8:34) δεξιᾷ

800   Lord κύριος

800   Omega ω

800   Master κύριος

800   Fidelity πίστις

800   Faith πίστις

800   Vermillion (red) שׁני

888   Jesus Ἰησους

8880   "Behold a virgin shall conceive and bear a son, and shall call his name Emmanuel, which being interpreted is, God with us." (Matt. 1:23) ἰδοὺ ἡ παρθένος ἐν γαστρὶ ἐξει καὶ τέξεται υἱόν, καὶ καλέσουσιν τὸ ὄνομα αὐτοῦ Ἐμμανουήλ, ὅ ἐστιν μεθερμηνευόμενον μεθ' ἡμῶν ὁ θεός.

888   "Salvation of our God" (Isa. 52:10) ישועת אלֹהֵינו

8880   "An ark, in which few, that is eight souls were saved through water." (I Pet. 3:20) κιβωτοῦ, εἰς ἣν ὀλίγοι, τοῦτ' ἔστιν ὀκτὼ ψυχαί, διεσώθησαν δι' ὕδατος.

888   "I am Jehovah, I change not" (Malachi 3:6) אני יהוה לא שניתי

808   Life ζάω

880   Sure (The foundation of God stands sure) (II Timothy 1:19) στερεὸς

880   Son (Romans 8:29) υἱοῦ

88   Victory νίκη

8 × 888   "The power of the most high will overshadow you, and the holy offspring will be called the Son of God." (Luke 1:35) δύναμις ὑψίστου ἐπισκιάσει σοι· διὸ καὶ τὸ γεννώμενον ἅγιον κληθήσεται υἱὸς θεοῦ.

8 × 888 "When the time had come, God sent forth His Son, born of a woman." (Gal. 4:4) οτε ἦλθεν πλήρωμα χρονου, ἐξαπεστειλεν θεος τον υιον αυτου, γενομενον εκ γυναικος

8888 "He must reign until he has put all enemies under his feet." (I Corinthians 15:25) δεῖ γαρ αυτον βασιλεύειν αχρι οὐ θῇ παντας τους ἐχθρους υπο τους πόδας αυτου.

8 The atomic number for oxygen.

The atomic weight of the hydrogen atom is given as 1.0080. The amazing gematria of this number results in the following:

1008 "The work of Thy fingers" (Psalm 8:3) מעשה אצבעתיך
1080 "Heaven is my throne and the earth is my footstool" (Isaiah 66:1) השמים כסאי האָרץ הדם רגלי
1080 "The Holy Spirit" (Mark 3:29) πνεῦμα το αγιον
108 Red חכלילי
1080 (Miles in the radius of the moon)
10080 (Miles in the combined diameters of the earth and moon)

The above demonstration of the work of the Creator leaves me humbled and without words. It is too marvelous for me. My mind is not able to absorb its magnificence. Now I know what the Apostle Paul must have felt when he exclaimed, *"O the depth of the riches both of the wisdom and knowledge of God! How unsearchable are his judgments, and his ways past finding out; for who hath known the mind of the Lord!"*

It was thrilling to observe the above relationship to the hydrogen atom, even to the fact that its characteristic color, red, bears its number both in the Hebrew and the Greek. Red is used in holy scripture as the symbol of the great work of the ransom for mankind and their ultimate redemption. That monumental work, the very basis and foundation of man's relationship with God, is exemplified by the power of the hydrogen atom.

The sun was god to many peoples throughout history because it was the source of light, warmth, and life. It glows red in the sky, and its brilliance is such that a man cannot look upon it, except as through the more dense atmospheric effect close to the horizon. It is indeed a fitting symbol of the true God.

The seemingly solid sun is actually a ball of gaseous plasma composed chiefly of hydrogen. It is in a constant state of fusion—producing the element helium. This fusion and resulting conversion to helium releases immense stores of heat and light. The effect of this thermonuclear fusion can be seen on the surface of the sun during the few seconds of a total solar eclipse.

Helium derives its name from the Greek word *helios,* which means sun. Not only its name, but its very existence is derived from the sun, being a product of the fusion of the sun's hydrogen. The atomic number for helium is 2.

The number 2 is also unique. It is the only number that can be derived solely from ones, as well as being the only prime number that is even. The numbers 1 and 2 are fitting symbols of the harmony and interrelationship of the Father and Son, and it is thrilling to find how the number 2 is used in the gematria of the Bible.

2000 Power of God ἐξουσία τοῦ θεοῦ
222 Jehovah God Most High (Genesis 14:22) יהוה אל עליון
222 I am Jehovah your God (Exodus 6:7) כי אני יהוה אלהיכם
220 High Priest (referring to Jesus Christ) (Hebrews 10:21) ἱερέα μέγαν
220 Lamb (the "Lamb of God," Jesus) פַּר
200 Divine (the nature of the Father and the Son) כסם
222 Nazarene (referring to Jesus) (Luke 4:34) Ναζαρηνε

Pythagoras and the Earth Model

Pythagoras taught that nature is commanded by numbers. The wonders of the above demonstration surely serve to confirm his convictions. Creation itself is commanded by numbers, and the Creator is the personification of those numbers.

When Pythagoras had proven his great theorem—the theorem of the right triangle—he offered a hundred oxen to the Muses in thanksgiving. What he experienced is such as every scientist or

15

physicists feels when the numbers say "this is a key to the structure of nature."

Pythagoras left for posterity the theorem of the right triangle. To him, the basic example of the right triangle in nature is the crossing of gravity with the horizon. He gave us the truth that the square on the hypotenuse of a triangle is equal to the squares of its two sides if, and only if, the angle they contain is a right angle: $a^2 + b^2 = c^2$. The simplest form of the right triangle is the 3:4:5 triangle which is found to be in complete harmony with nature and the universe because $3 + 4 + 5 = 12$, the foundation number. Pythagoras had found a great truth, but the application of it was planted in the universe from the beginning of creation.

If a model of the moon were placed tangent to a model of the earth, and squares drawn on the diameters of the circles, the model would look like this:

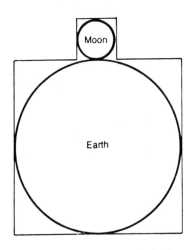

Next, let's place the distances (in miles) on the model. Pythagoras probably did not do this because the dimensions of earth and moon were not then known.

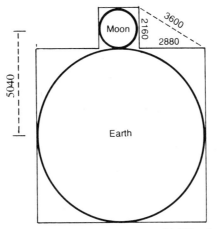

Perimeter of joining squares, 36,000 miles

Note that the right triangle formed by the placement of the squares is a perfect 3:4:5 triangle. It was not the work of Pythagoras; it was the work of the Creator. The actual dimensions of the triangle are:

$$3 = 2160 \text{ miles}$$
$$4 = 2880 \text{ miles}$$
$$5 = 3600 \text{ miles}$$

If the diameter of the earth were used as the base of a pyramid, and the center of the moon as the apex, the proportions of that pyramid would be the exact proportions of the Great Pyramid in Egypt, having a base angle of 51° 51 ′.

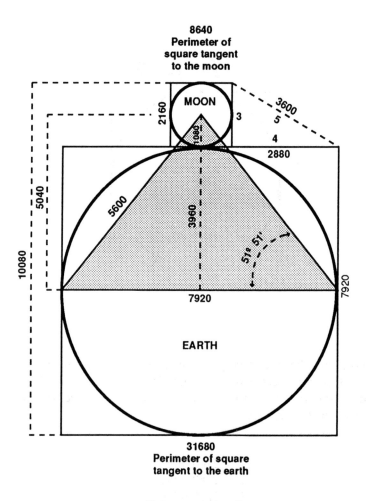

Distances are in miles.

18

The numbers produced by this model bear an astonishing relationship to the gematria of the Bible. Note its reference to God as the Creator, to Jesus as the Redeemer, and to the Kingom of God as universal.

2160 Diameter of moon
2160 Kingdom of the Father (Matt. 13:43) $\beta\alpha\sigma\iota\lambda\epsilon\dot{\iota}\alpha\ \tau\hat{\omega}\nu\ \pi\alpha\tau\rho\dot{o}s$
216 Mighty נְבוּרָה
216 Power נְבוּרָה

1080 Radius of moon
1080 The Holy Spirit $\pi\nu\epsilon\hat{v}\mu\alpha\ \tau o\ \alpha\gamma\iota o\nu$
1080 Heaven is my throne and the earth is my footstool
       השמים כסאי והארץ הדם רגלי (Isaiah 66:1)

8640 Perimeter of a square on the diameter of moon
864 He shall reign (Rev. 11:15) $\beta\alpha\sigma\iota\lambda\epsilon\acute{v}\sigma\epsilon\iota$
864 Holy of holies $\alpha\gamma\iota\omega\nu$
864 Saints $\alpha\gamma\iota\omega\nu$
864 Jerusalem 'Ι$\epsilon\rho o\nu\sigma\alpha\lambda\eta\mu$
864 Life $\zeta\omega\acute{\eta}\nu$

7920 Diameter of earth
792 You made him to rule (Psalm 8:7) תמשילהי
       (This is a statement concerning man's dominion.)
792 Jehovah made the heavens (Psalm 96:5) ויהוה שמים עשה

3960 Radius of earth
396 On the earth (Gen. 1:15) על־הארץ
396 The heavens (Isa. 40:12) ישמים

31680 Perimeter of a square drawn on the diameter of earth
3168 Lord Jesus Christ Κ$\nu\rho\iota os$ 'Ι$\eta\sigma o\nu s$ Χ$\rho\iota\sigma\tau os$

2880 Base of the 3:4:5 triangle
2880 Kingom of heaven (Matt. 13:47) $\beta\alpha\sigma\iota\lambda\epsilon\acute{\iota}\alpha\ \tau\hat{\omega}\nu\ o\dot{v}\rho\alpha\nu\hat{\omega}\nu$

19

3600 Hypotenuse of the 3:4:5 triangle
360   Number of degrees in a circle, symbol of everlastingness
3600 The Lamb's book of life (Rev. 21:27) τῷ βιβλίῳ ζωῆς ἀρνίου.
360   The Rock that begat us (Deut. 32:18) צוּר יְלָדְךָ
36   God (Elah) אֱלָה

5040 Combined radii of earth and moon
5040 The Kingdom of our Lord and His Christ (Rev. 11:15)
      βασιλεια κυριου ημων και Χριστου αυτου'

10080 Combined diameters of earth and moon
1008 "The work of thy fingers" (Psalm 8:3) מעשה אצבעתיך
1.0080 Atomic weight of the hydrogen atom

The pyramid that has been superimposed on the model has sides
of 5600. It fits the picture beautifully to find the gematria of
everlasting   יוֹם   to be 56, forever   יוֹם   56, Golden City מרהבה
56, and 'The Saints of the Most High" (Daniel 7:18) קַדִּישֵׁי עֶלְיוֹנִין,
560.

The evidence is overwhelming! The universe is indeed commanded by numbers, and the Creator so designed it to show his plan for
the salvation of man through Jesus Christ, and his ultimate blessing of them in his Kingdom of Peace.

The superimposing of the Great Pyramid on the earth-moon
model reveals many things. That mysterious ancient structure,
standing its lonely vigil over the Nile delta, plays an integral role
in the plan of God. Indeed its stones cry out to be heard.

2

The Stones
of The Great Pyramid

The Great Pyramid is the oldest wonder of the world. All the generations of man have marveled at its construction and searched for its origin and purpose. This ancient wonder continues to be a modern mystery.

The enormous size of that ancient structure is difficult to comprehend, even when standing beside its base and traversing its magnificent mass with our eyes. Its base covers 13 acres. It contains enough masonry to build a sidewalk three inches thick and two feet wide that would reach around the world. It rises to a height of 485 feet[1] —comparable to the height of a 40-story building. Built of solid limestone throughout, except for its chambers and passage systems, clearly, whoever built the Great Pyramid wanted it to remain. And remain it has!

The Great Pyramid was once covered with dazzling white casing stones which could be seen from great distances because it captured and reflected the sun's rays. The ancient Strabo said it was "like a building let down from heaven, untouched by human hands."

Herodotus, who has been called "The Father of History," saw the Great Pyramid in 440 B.C. He recorded that each side of the structure was covered with highly polished white limestone, with joints so fine they could scarcely be seen.

---

(1) This measurement includes the topstone which was apparently never placed.

Modern theory suggests that the Great Pyramid was a tomb. However, historians are nearly all in agreement that no one was ever buried there. Many suppose it to have been built for the purpose of entombing the body of the Egyptian king Cheops, but Egyptologists tell us that he was buried in an elaborately-cut sepulcher about a thousand feet away from the Pyramid.

In A.D. 820 the Caliph Al Mamoun and his workmen forced an entrance into the sealed Pyramid. Finally, after weeks of difficult labor, they broke into a dark passageway. The pounding of their hammers accidentally dislodged a large limestone block that had sealed and hidden a passage that led upward. They were the first men ever to traverse those upper passages and chambers, which had obviously been sealed since the time of construction. Not only had they been sealed by the limestone block, but additionally by three gigantic tightly fitting granite blocks which exactly filled the whole lower end of the first ascending passage, completely blocking it. Those granite "plugs" remain in the passage to this day,

The front, or north face of the Great Pyramid.

and visitors to the Pyramid must use the forced passage created by Al Mamoun.

Clearly, no one had ever gone in or out of the upper passage system from the time of its construction. Yet, when Al Mamoun and his workmen explored the upper passages and chambers, they found no mummy, nor any evidence that one had ever been there.

In the uppermost chamber, known today as the King's Chamber, they found a lidless, open, empty granite box. The box was larger than could have been brought through the passage system. It was obviously placed there by the builders, and the chamber constructed around it as the Pyramid was being built upward. Had it ever contained a mummy or a lid they could not have been removed because of the small places in the passage and the impenetrable granite plugs.

If that gigantic stone monument was not a tomb, what was it?

In 1868 the Chief Hydrographer of the United States Coastal Survey, Henry Mitchell, was awed by the remarkable shape of the

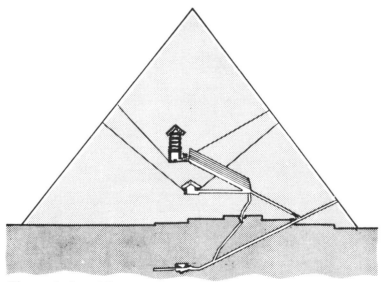

The vertical meridian section of the Great Pyramid, showing its passage and chamber system.

23

Nile Delta. He observed that the regularity of the general curvature of the coast of the delta forms a quadrant. This led him to wonder what point marked the focal point of the quadrant, and thus the center of the circle. To his amazement, he found the Great Pyramid sitting on the precise spot. With this discovery he exclaimed, "That monument stands in a more important physical situation than any other building erected by man."

What Mitchell had discovered had been written more than 2,500 years previously by the prophet Isaiah:

> *In that day shall there be an altar to the Lord in the midst of the land of Egypt, and a pillar* (Hebrew "Matstsebah"— monument) *at the border thereof to the Lord. And it shall be for a sign, and for a witness unto the Lord of Hosts in the land of Egypt.* (Isaiah 19:19-20)

There is only one spot on the face of the earth that fits Isaiah's description, and on that spot the Great Pyramid stands.

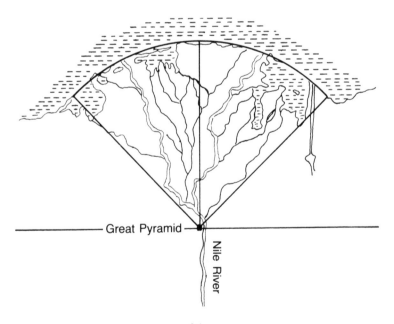

Great Pyramid

Nile River

STONES OF THE GREAT PYRAMID

Commenting on Mitchell's discovery, Professor C. Piazzi Smyth, Astronomer Royal for Scotland, said:

Now Lower Egypt being as already described, of a sector, still more exactly than of a Delta shape, it must have its centre, not like a circle in the middle of its surface, but at one extreme corner thereof. Whereupon Mr. Mitchell has acutely remarked that the building which stands at, or just raised above, such a *sectorial* centre must be at one and the same time both at the border thereof, and yet at its *quasi,* or practically governing, middle. That is to say, just as was to be that grandly honored prophetic monument, pure and undefiled in its religious bearing, though in an idolatrous Egyptian land, alluded to by Isaiah (Chapter 19); for was it not fore-ordained by the Divine Word to be both *"an altar to the Lord in the midst of the land of Egypt, and a pillar at the border thereof"*—an apparent mechanical impossibility, yet realised in the sectorial centre condition of the Great Pyramid.

However, O. deBlaere, of Antwerp, Belgium was the first to point out that the gematria of this statement by Isaiah describes the Great Pyramid and none other. Adding the number equivalents for the entire two verses, he found the total numeric value to be 5,449. The actual height of the Great Pyramid, from base to the summit platform, as left by the builders, is 5,449 Pyramid inches.[1]

In the year 1865 Professor C. Piazzi Smyth took measurements of the Great Pyramid. On the basis of those measurements he was able to determine that π (3.14159) and y (365.242) constitute the basis of the Pyramid's construction: the value of y being the number of days in the solar tropical year. At that time, the base of the Pyramid lay buried under huge piles of sand and debris, making an accurate measurement not possible. However, he computed the base perimeter on the constructural basis of π and $y,$ and suggested that the base side length would be 365.242 sacred cubits,

---

(1) The Pyramid inch was a unit of measure in the structural design of the Great Pyramid. It is described as 1 Pyramid inch equals 1.00106 British inches or 1 British inch equals .99894 of a Pyramid inch.

ביום	58
ההוא	17
יהיה	30
מזבח	57
ליהוה	56
בתוך	428
ארץ	291
מצרים	380
ומצבה	143
אצל	121
גבולה	46
ליהוה	56
והיה	26
לאות	437
ולעד	110
ליהוה	56
צבאות	499
בארץ	293
מצרים	380
כי	30
יצעקו	276
אל	31
יהוה	26
מפני	180
לחצים	178
וישלח	354
להם	75
מושיע	426
ורב	208
והצילם	181

Height of the Great Pyramid in Pyramid inches, to the original summit platform . . . . 5,449 or the number of sacred cubits as there are days required for the earth to orbit the sun.

Many years later, after the rubble had been cleared away, modern surveys were undertaken and an accurate measurement could be obtained. The results were startling! They uncovered rectangular sockets beneath each of the four corners, and the survey showed that the original full design of the structure did indeed have a base side length of 365.242 sacred cubits, giving a total base perimeter of 36524.2 Pyramid inches.

The Great Pyramid and the Earth Model

During the clearing away of the debris from the base of the Pyramid, a few of the original smoothly polished white casing stones were found, still entact. These huge angular limestone blocks were a most valuable discovery, for by their angle we are

Photo courtesy Todd Alexander, Pyramid Productions, Inc.

Nearly all of the Great Pyramid's beautiful white casing stones have been stripped from its sides to build the capital city of El Kaherah. The size of these huge stones can be appreciated in relation to the size of the man standing beside them.

able to determine the original height of the Pyramid. The angle was found to be 51° 51'. Those who discovered this angle were not

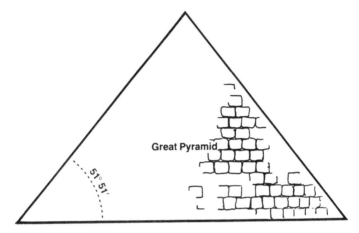

aware of its importance in the understanding of the origin and purpose of the monument. They did not know that the Great Pyramid angle, 51° 51', was planted by the Creator in the relationship of earth to earth's moon.

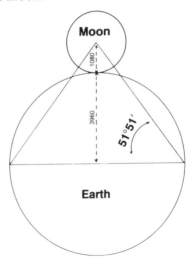

Such evidence confirms the speculation that the Creator of the earth and moon was also involved in the design of the Great Pyramid, for the size of the earth and the moon were not known to man at the time of the building of that magnificent monument.

When the Pyramid model is constructed on the earth-moon model, some remarkable facts come to view.

The diameter of the earth (7,920 miles) becomes the base of the projected pyramid, thus the base perimeter of this earth-commensurate pyramid is 31,680 miles. We have already noted that the name Lord Jesus Christ Κυριος Ιησους Χριστος, has a number equivalent of 3168. The implication is obvious: that Pyramid, built in the land of Egypt, built on the geometry of the earth and moon, has a foundation which represents the great work of redemption accomplished by the Lord Jesus Christ.

The height of each side of this earth-commensurate pyramid becomes 5,600 miles. The figure represents everlasting life as becomes obvious from its gematria in scripture:

56   everlasting יום
56   forever יום
56   Golden City מדהבה
560 Blessed be Jehovah my Rock (Psalm 144:1) בָּרוּךְ יהוה צוּרִי
560 The saints of the Most High (Daniel 7:18) קְדִישֵׁי עֶלְיוֹנִין

The vertical height of the earth-commensurate pyramid becomes 5,040 miles. The figure depicts the completed work of redemption as embodied in the long-promised kingdom.

5040 The Kingdom of our Lord and His Christ (Revelation 11:15)
       βασιλεια κυριου ημων και Χριστου αυτου'

This 5,040 miles is composed of the earth radius of 3,960 miles and the moon radius of 1,080 miles. The figure 396 and 1080 embody the concept of heaven and earth—the completed plan of God.

396   Heaven (Isaiah 66:1) השמים
396   the heavens (Isaiah 40:12) ושמים
396   on the earth (Genesis 1:15) על־הארץ
1080 Heaven is my throne and the earth is my footstool
       (Isaiah 66:1) השמים כסאי והארץ הדם רגלי

THE STONES CRY OUT

The topstone of the Great Pyramid

The only stone in the Great Pyramid that was in itself a perfect pyramid would have been the topstone. This massive stone was never placed on the summit; however, it was undoubtedly in existence, and used as a model in the shaping of the casing stones to the required angle.

Theory has it that the topstone was covered with gold. Considering this possibility, the noted pyramidologist, Adam Rutherford exclaimed:

> . . . what a Topstone! Think of its gigantic size, its tremendous weight and the fabulous cost of gold to cover such a colossal Crowning Stone! Picture, in the brilliant sunshine, this great Top-Stone, arrayed in gold, in itself a perfect pyramid of dazzling brillance, towering high on the lofty summit of the massive Pyramid of snowy white—supreme magnificence indeed . . . ![1]

Rutherford, however, was only creating a beautiful picture in the mind, because he elsewhere stated that this beautiful topstone had never been placed.[2]

The suggestion that it was covered with gold is a fitting picture, for there is evidence that this massive angular stone beautifully pictured the completed work of redemption as represented in the Lord Jesus Christ.

If indeed it had been covered with gold (or perhaps one day will be covered with gold), it would bear the number of man's redeemer. The prophet Isaiah looked forward to the birth of that redeemer when he said, *"Behold, a virgin shall conceive, and bear a son, and shall call his name Immanuel."* And the gospel writer, Matthew, said this was prophetic of the birth of Jesus. The name Immanuel עמנו אל , by gematria, bears the number 197. The atomic weight of gold is 197.

---

(1) Adam Rutherford, *Pyramidology Book II,* Institute of Pyramidology, London, 1962, p. 259.

(2) *Ibid.,* p. 233

This topstone, with which the workmen were familiar, but which was never placed atop the structure, is alluded to in many places in holy scripture.

The stone which the builders refused is become the headstone of the corner. This is the Lord's doing; it is marvelous in our eyes. (Psalm 118:22, 23)

Be it known unto you all, and to all the people of Israel, that by the name of Jesus Christ of Nazareth, whom ye crucified, whom God raised from the dead, even by him doth this man stand here before you whole. This is the stone which was set at nought of you builders, which is become the head of the corner. Neither is there salvation in any other: for there is none other name under heaven given among men, whereby we must be saved. (Acts 4:10-12)

Wherefore also it is contained in scripture, Behold, I lay in Zion a chief cornerstone, elect, precious: and he that believeth on him shall not be confounded. Unto you therefore which believe he is precious: but unto them which be disobedient, the stone which the builders disallowed, the same is made the head of the corner. (I Peter 2:6, 7)

Therefore thus saith the Lord God, Behold, I lay in Zion for a foundation a stone, a tried stone, a precious cornerstone, a sure foundation. (Isaiah 28:16)

This glorious topstone, a perfect pyramid, had a base perimeter of 2288.8 Pyramid inches (or nearly 48 feet per side), and a height of 364.27 Pyramid inches (or about 30 feet). No wonder it was never lifted into place on that lofty summit—its mass, as one piece of hewn rock, was gigantic!

Had it ever been placed, and had it indeed have been covered with gold, surely it would have shone magnificently as the sun and its beauty and brilliance would have been seen throughout all the surrounding country.

Perhaps it was meant to be a symbol of the sun, for the reference to this beautiful stone in I Peter 2:6 calls it γωνία, (topstone) and it has a number equivalent of 864. The diameter of the sun is

864,000 miles.

The scriptural references to this topstone speak of it as representing the Lord Jesus Christ, and it is not surprising that its geometry and gematria confirm it.

2288.8 Pyramid inches - base perimeter of the topstone
2288   Christ the Lord, Χριστος Κυριος
       (while 8 represents the resurrection and a new beginning.)

111 Royal cubits - base perimeter of the topstone
111   Wonderful (Isaiah 9:6) פלא
1110 The root of Jesse (referring to Jesus) (Isaiah 11:10) יש שרש
11   Gold דהב

14.6 Sacred cubits - height of the topstone
146   A precious cornerstone, a sure foundation (Isaiah 28:16)
       פנת יקרת מוסד מוסד
146   everlasting עולם

37 Sacred cubits - combined height of 2 angled sides of topstone
370   perfect שלם
370   great power עריץ
370   to reign משל
370   to make restitution שלם
370   ruler מֹשֵל
370   glory הכבוד

74 Sacred cubits - combined height of 4 angled sides of topstone
74   foundation יסד
74   redeemer (Psalm 78:35) גאלם
74   a great God (Psalm 95:3) אל ָ:־יל

810 British inches - diagonal of base of topstone
810   Advocate παρακλητος
810   Comforter παρακλητος
810   friend φιλος

32

53 headstone אבן
53 sun חמה
53 Son υιον
530 cornerstone פנה
5300 his life a ransom for many (Matthew 20:28)
    ψυχὴν αὐτοῦ λύτρον ἀντὶ πολλῶν.

The scriptural record and the gematria make it quite clear—the topstone is indeed a figure of Jesus. However, to further prove the correctness of this concept, I tried a little mathematical game. Using the proportions of the topstone and the Pyramid angle of 51° 51 ′ 14.3 ″ I constructed 100 triangles (mathematically of course) using random numbers. Then I tried the same thing, using the numbers that are the gematria for the names of Jesus or pertain to his work, as man's redeemer. The triangles constructed with random numbers produced dimensions with no apparent significance; however, when I used numbers relating to Jesus, the results appeared to have been the intentional design of the architect. The demonstration below would be amazing indeed, had it been merely coincidental.

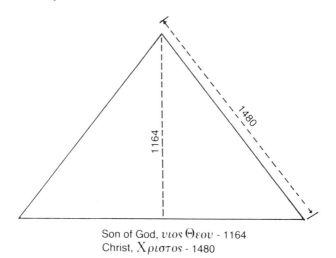

Son of God, υιος Θεου - 1164
Christ, Χριστος - 1480

THE STONES CRY OUT

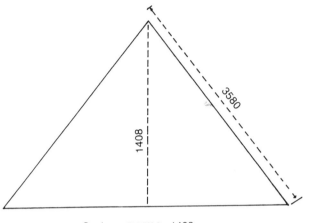

Saviour, σωτηρ - 1408
Messiah, משיח - 358

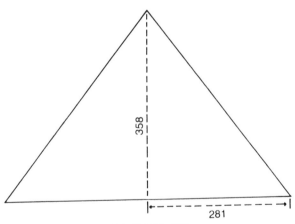

Messiah, משיח - 358
Lamb, αρνιον - 281

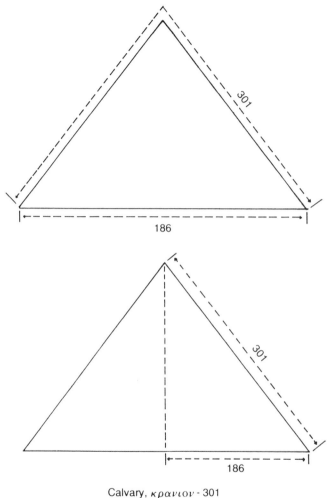

Calvary, κρανιον - 301
Golgotha, Γολγοθα - 186

The illustration on page 18 showed the construction of the Great Pyramid on the geometric proportion of earth and moon. Note that in the illustration, the apex, or topstone of the Pyramid reaches exactly to the center of the moon. The figure 2160 is the lunar number, being the number of miles in its diameter. I believe it to be the intent of the Architect to point directly to the One whom the topstone represents, for it is recorded in Matthew 21:42 *"The stone which the builders rejected, the same is become the head of the corner: this is the Lord's doing, and it is marvelous in our eyes."*

2,160 miles - diameter of the moon
2160 The stone which the builders rejected λίθον ον
      απεδοκίμασαν οι οικοδομοῦντες

It was indeed the plan of the Creator from the beginning.

The Interior of the Great Pyramid

The tomb theory had its origins in the many other pyramids in Egypt which were indeed tombs, their burial chambers having been observed and studied by archaeologists. Noting this, Joseph A. Seiss, in his *Miracle in Stone*[1] made the following observation:

> The truth is that the tomb theory does not fit the facts, the traditions, or any knowledge that we have on the subject. It is wholly borrowed from the numerous later pyramids, ambitiously and ignorantly copied after it, which were intended and used for royal sepulchres, but with which the Great Pyramid has nothing in common, save locality and general shape. In all the examination to which it has been subjected, whether in ancient or modern times, and in all the historic fragments concerning it, there is nothing whatever to give or to bear out the idea that its intention was that of a royal sepulchral monument . . .

The "numerous later pyramids" to which Seiss made reference, are about thirty-eight in all, and they dot the western side of the Nile along the edge of the great Sahara Desert. All of them are square-based, with four triangular sloping sides, meeting at the top in a point over the center of the base. Many of them have long since collapsed into rounded ruins and are no longer recognizable as pyramids. However, they all, with the exception of the Great Pyramid alone, have no upper passages and chambers.

(1) Joseph A. Seiss, *Miracle in Stone,* The Castle Press, Philadelphia, 1877, p. 185.

STONES OF THE GREAT PYRAMID

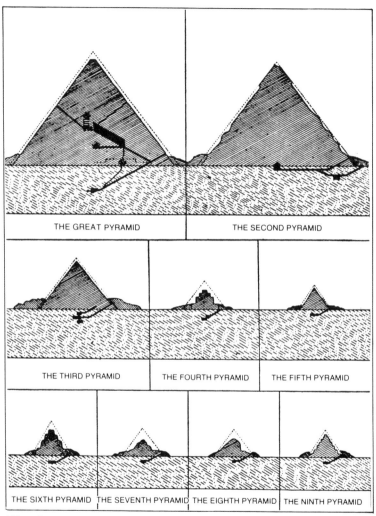

The above is an adaptation of the drawings of Piazzi Smyth showing the vertical meridian section of the nine pyramids of Gizeh. Note that all have descending passages, but the Great Pyramid, alone, has ascending passages. These upper passages were sealed and hidden by the builders, hence those who attempted to copy the design knew only of the descending passage.

Why, if they had been copied from the idea of the Great Pyramid, would they not have upper passages and chambers? The reason is obvious. The upper passage system of the Great Pyramid was sealed and concealed by the builders—no one knew it was there. Not until the pounding of the hammers of Al Mamoun's workmen, in A.D. 820, dislodged the stone that concealed the passage, did anyone ever know of its upper passage and chamber system.

Since that great discovery, men have explored its interior with continued awe and amazement. The design of its passages and chambers reveals the precision of an architect with a purpose. Those who first measured its interior expressed great wonder at the precise angle of ascent and descent of its passages. The precision was obvious—they all bore the same steep angle, 26° 18 '9.7".

The architect who designed the passages displayed a remarkable knowledge of mathematics. The sine of this angle is equal to the square root of π divided by 4.

$$\text{sine of } 26° \ 18' \ 9.7" = .4431135$$
$$\frac{\sqrt{\pi}}{4} = .4431135$$

This unique angle of 26° 18 ' 9.7 "is earth commensurate. This is shown by the simple geometrical demonstration below. Consider two earth-diameters as the length of one side of a square. Then inscribe a circle within the square. Now square the circle (circle and square of equal area). The resultant square will measure 14037.8 units. Now stack the squares in the manner shown below, and the angle created is precisely the Pyramid passage angle— 26° 18 ' 9.7".

Unmistakably, the Pyramid passage angle, like its outer base-to-apex angle, was designed on the diameter of the earth. But notice the numbers in its base and hypotenuse—3168 and 284. The name Lord Jesus Christ in Greek is Κυριος Ἰησους Χριστος and has the number equivalent of 3168, and God is Θεος and

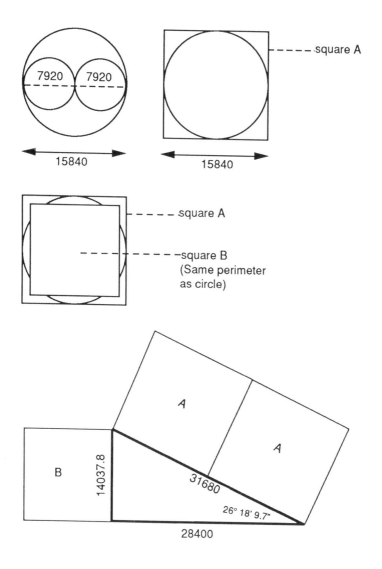

bears the number 284. A fact beyond the reach of coincidence!
The evidence of divine intervention and direction in the construction of the Great Pyramid is remarkable. But why? What was

the purpose for constructing that massive pile of stones—a structure so enduring that it remains to this day. After 4,000 years of the extremes of a desert location, after 4,000 years of the vandalism of man, after 4,000 years of natural destructive forces, the Great Pyramid stands bold and silent and enduring.

Perhaps a clue to the intent of the architect can be found in those verses already alluded to in Isaiah 19:19-20, which so clearly describe the location of the Great Pyramid. Isaiah said it would "become a sign and a witness to the Lord of hosts in the land of Egypt."

Has it? A sign of what? A witness to what?

Those three questions can now be answered plainly. The answer to the first is yes. Question number two: it has become a sign of a great plan of the Creator involving the salvation of man; and three—it is a witness to the very existence of God.

Within the past two centuries, much has been written regarding this witness, and lifetimes have been devoted to its study.[1] One predominant observation has been threaded through all their works—that monument stands as a witness to a grand and glorious plan involving the destiny of man.

In the year 1877, Joseph A. Seiss, D.D., Pastor of the Church of the Holy Communion in Philadelphia, Pennsylvania wrote:[2]

> If the half that learned and scientific investigators allege respecting the Great Pyramid of Gizeh be true, it is one of the most interesting objects on earth, and ought to command universal attention . . . . Simply as an architectural achievement, this mysterious pillar . . . has held its place at the head of the list of "The Seven Wonders of the World." But, under the researches and studies of mathematicians, astronomers,

---

1 I do not attempt a complete list for fear of leaving someone out, however, a few are as follows:
Morton Edgar, *The Great Pyramid*
Adam Rutherford, *Pyramidology*
Joseph A. Seiss, *Miracle in Stone*
Piazzi Smyth, *The Great Pyramid, its secrets and mysteries revealed*
John Taylor, *The Great Pyramid: why was it built and who built it?*

2 *Joseph A. Seiss, Miracle in Stone,* The Castle Press, Philadelphia, 1877, p. 3.

Egyptologists . . . it has . . . a character vastly more remarkable. Facts . . . so numerous and extraordinary have been evolved, that some of the most sober and philosophic minds have been startled by them. It would verily seem . . . to prove itself a sort of key to the universe—a symbol of the profoundest truths, of sciences, of religion, and of all the past and future history of man.

Indeed it has proven to be a key to the universe and a symbol of the profoundest truths regarding the future of man. It tells the same story as the Bible. Some have called it the Bible written in stone. It tells of the disobedience of Adam (original sin) and the subsequent downward course of the human family toward death—represented by the Descending Passage leading to the Pit. It tells of a way of life offered through the Mosaic Law—a way not only opened by but also blocked by the law, as represented by the First Ascending Passage with its impenetrable and immovable Granite Plugs, prohibiting all entrance. It tells of the free gift of life provided by the ransom sacrifice of Jesus as represented by the Well. It tells of a kingdom on earth, where God's will is done, even as it is done in heaven—represented by the Queen's Chamber with its life-giving air vents. It tells of the walk of the Christian toward a heavenly goal—represented by the beautiful but steep Grand Gallery. And it tells of the heavenly administration of Christ's Kingdom as represented by the King's Chamber.

This Pyramid, whose construction was based on the dimensions of earth and moon, is the embodiment of the long-promised Kingdom of our Lord and His Christ. As we have seen in the earth-moon model on page 18, the pyramid constructed on the radii of earth and moon, had a height of 5040 miles, and the gematria for *"The Kingdom of our Lord and His Christ"* (Revelation 11:15) is exactly 5040.

The actual height of the Great Pyramid of Gizeh, to the top of its headstone is 485 + feet. That most remarkable pile of rock on the face of the earth bears the number 485 from its base to its apex—and the Bible so beautifully tells us *"There is no rock like our God,"* (I Samuel 2:2). That profound statement in gematria bears the number 485. Surely that most enduring monument of all history is the very embodiment of the Creator and his plan for the salvation of his human family.

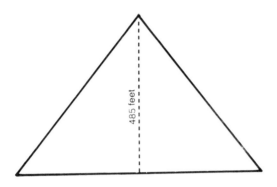

485 feet = full height of Great Pyramid
485 = "There is no Rock like our God" (I Samuel 2:2)

When Jesus rode into Jerusalem on that unforgettable day in A.D. 33, he exclaimed to those who rebuked the shouting, *"If these should hold their peace, the stones would immediately cry out."* The greatest pile of stones the earth has ever known has not held its peace—it has been crying out since time immemorial that there is a God. It has been crying out that a grand master plan for man's redemption through Jesus Christ had been formed from the beginning, and has been in progress throughout the ages. The grand fulfillment of that plan involves the complete reconciliation between God and his human family in a Kingdom of peace.

3

The Circle of Stones

Throughout history, men have placed stones in the configuration of a circle. The idea conveyed by the figure of a circle is everlastingness. Just as a circle has no beginning nor ending, so is the concept of eternity. It is the symbol that refers to the Creator.

The word *circle, κυκλos,* as used in the New Testament Scriptures has a number equivalent of 740. It is not only a fundamental principle of geometry and mathematics, it is also a fundamental concept of creation. In fact, the word *creation, κτιοιs,* also bears the number, by gematria, of 740 as does the word *foundation* יסד .

74, that great foundation number, reveals its meaning by gematria:

74 eternity עד

74 everlasting עד

74 foundation יסד

74 witness עד

740 "you have laid the foundation of the earth" (Psalm 102:25)
      יסדת הארץ

740 creation κτιοιs

740 circle κυκλos

740 great stones ποταποὶ λίθοι

74 a great God אל גדיל

740 His delight שעשעי

74 their redemption גאלם

740 "for He will hide me in his shelter in the day of evil" (Psalm 27:5) כי יצפני בסכה ביום רעה

43

That a circle is related to things everlasting is indellibly shown by the following demonstration of gematria: 74 = circle.

74 × 2 = 148

148   victory נצח

148   The Branch (referring prophetically to Jesus) (Zechariah 3:8) צמח

148   blood (the price of man's redemption) נצח

1480   Christ Χριστος

1480   Kingdom of God (Matthew 6:33) βασιλείαν αὐτοῦ

1480   make strong στεριow

1480   establish στεριow

148   The Most High God (Daniel 4:2) אלהא עליא

74 × 3 = 222

222   Jehovah God Most High (Gen. 14:22) יהוה אל עליון

222   I am Jehovah your God (Exodus 6:7) כי אני יהוה אלהיכם

2220   I am Alpha and Omega (Rev. 1:11) ἐγὼ αλφα καὶ ωμεγα

222   The Lord is my strength (rock) and my shield (Psalm 28:7) יהוה עזי ומגני

222   Nazarene (referring to Jesus) (Luke 4:34) Ναζαρηνέ

222   a stone of stumbling (referring to Jesus) (Isaiah 8:14) ולאבן נגף

74 × 4 = 296

296   God צור

296   mighty one צור

296   strength צור

296   only begotten (referring to Jesus) μονογενη

296   stone צור

296   the earth (Psalm 96:1) הארץ

296   water from the rock (prophetic of the blood of Christ) (Nehemiah 9:15) ומים מסלע

2960   eternal salvation σωτηρίας αἰωνίου

2960   Son of Man (one of the titles of Jesus) o υιος ανθρωπου

$74 \times 5 = 370$

(37 and 2 are the prime factors of 74, thus 37 is a factor of all the multiples of 74.)

370 peace שלם

370 perfect שלם

370 great power עריץ

370 to reign מָשַׁל

370 to make restitution (the work of Jesus) שלם

370 to restore שלם

370 to rule משל

370 ruler משל

370 whole שלם

370 whole ὅλος (both the Hebrew and Greek words for "whole" bear the same number.)

370 temple οικος

370 your heavens (Psalm 8:4) שמיך

37 God (Daniel 4:2) אלהא

37 glory הכבוד

37 strength אגל

37 heart לבה

$74 \times 6 = 444$

444 holy place מקדש

444 sanctuary מקדש

4440 the Lord Christ (Col. 3:24) τῷ κυρίῳ Χριστῷ

4440 "the temple of God was opened in heaven" (Rev. 11:19)
ἠνοίγη ὁ ναὸς τοῦ θεοῦ ὁ ἐν τῷ οὐρανῷ

$74 \times 8 = 592$

592 Godhead θεοτης

592 holiness ἁγιοτης

592 "and the stone shall become the house of God (referring to the Bethel stone which represented Christ) (Gen. 28:22)
והאבן יהיה בית אלהים

45

74 × 12 = 888

888   Jesus ᾽Ιησους

888   The Founder ὁ οἰκιστης,

888   I am the Life εἰμι ἡ ζωή

888   Salvation of our God   ישועת אלהינו

888   I am Jehovah, I change not (Mal. 3:6)   אני יהוה לא שניתי

8880   An ark, in which few, that is eight souls were saved through water. (The ark pictured Christ) (I Peter 3:20) κιβωτου εις ην ολιγοι τουτ εστιν οκτω ψυχαι διεσωθησαν δι υδατος

8880   Behold a virgin shall conceive and bear a son, and shall call his name Emmanuel, which being interpreted is, God with us. (Matt. 5:23) ιδου η παρθενος εν γαστρι εξει και τεξεται υιον και καλεσουσν ονομα αυτου Εμμανουηλ ο εστιν μεθερμηνευομενον μεθ ημων Θεος

74 × 15 = 1110

1110   The root of Jesse (referring to Jesus) (Isaiah 11:10) שרש ישי

111   The Most High (Daniel 4:32) עליא

111   Wonderful (prophetic of Jesus) (Isaiah 9:6) פלא

111   house (my Father's house) (John 14:2) οἰκία

74 × 18 = 1332

1332   The Child Jesus το παιδιον Ιησουν᾽

74 × 24 = 1776

1776   Lord of the sabbath κύριός σαββάτου

1776   Jesus of Nazareth (1777) ᾽Ιησου Ναζωραιον

74 × 25 = 1850

185   Rabbi (referring to Jesus) ο ραββι

74 × 27 = 1998

1998   The name of Jesus (1999) ονοματι του Ιησου

1998   I am the son of God (1999) υιος του Θεου ειμι

74 × 32 = 2368

2368 Jesus Christ Ἰησους Χριστος
2368 Holy of holies ο αγιος των αγιων
2368 The God of Gods ο Θεοσ των Θεων

74 × 33 = 2442

2442 The son of God τη υιου του Θεου
2442 Jesus, the name given by the angel
      Ιησους το κληθεν υπο αγγελου

74 × 35 = 2590

259 Kingom (Jesus was the personification of the Kingdom of
    God) βασιλεία

74 × 36 = 2664

2664 The Lord God is one Lord κυριος Θεος κυριος εις εστιν

74 × 45 = 3330

333 Thy throne O God is forever (Psalm 45:6) כסאך אלהים ייים

74 × 48 = 3552

3552 Author of eternal salvation αιτιος σωτηριας αιωνιου

74 × 75 = 5550

555 Our Lord and His Christ κυριου ημων και του χριστου αυτου
555 The face of the sanctuary ופני הקדש
555 power (Mark 12:24) δύναμιν

74 × 90 = 6660

666 The head of the corner (referring to Christ as the topstone of
    the Pyramid.) לראש פנה

74 × 105 = 7770

777 the Man Child (Rev. 12:13) τον αρσενα.

The Twelve Stones of Gilgal

The story of the Hebrew people in the Old Testament is a fascinating one. Students of the Old Testament find in the experiences of those people many prophetic illustrations. Many of the things that God instructed them to do had a deeper meaning than may have appeared to the people at the time. One such story was the crossing of the Jordan River.

After fleeing Egyptian bondage, under the leadership of Moses, the Israelites wandered as nomads, without a land they could call their own, for a space of forty years. After the death of Moses, their newly appointed leader, Joshua, was instructed by God to bring the people across the River Jordan and into the land that had been promised to them for a possession.

God instructed Joshua to appoint twelve men, one from each of the twelve tribes, to take a stone from the middle of the Jordan and bring it to shore on the other side. These were no small stones, for the instruction was for each man to carry it upon his shoulder.

The stones were carried to a small hill and there placed in a circle. They were to be for a memorial of their deliverance from Egypt, from their homeless wandering in the wilderness, and the miraculous crossing of the Jordan on dry land (for God had parted the waters as he had done previously at the Red Sea).

And Joshua said unto them, Pass over before the Ark of the Lord your God into the midst of the Jordan, and take you up every man a stone upon his shoulder, according to the number of the tribes of the children of Israel: that this may be a sign among you, that when your children ask their fathers in time to come, saying, What mean ye by these stones? Then ye shall answer them, that the waters of Jordan were cut off before the Ark of the Covenant of the Lord; when it passed over Jordan, the waters of the Jordan were cut off: and these stones shall be for a memorial unto the children of Israel forever. . .that all the people of the earth might know the hand of the Lord, that it is mighty; that ye might fear the Lord your God forever. (Joshua 4:5-24)

And the Lord said unto Joshua, this day have I rolled away

the reproach of Egypt from off you. Wherefore the name of
the place is called Gilgal unto this day. (Joshua 5:9)

That statement was a play on words, which is quite often found in the Old Testament record. The word Gilgal literally means a wheel or that which is circular, but it was also used to mean "rolling away," or a "whirlwind."

The "rolling away" of the reproach of Egypt, and the placing of the stones in a circle as a wheel, appropriately gave the place the name of Gilgal.

The twelve stones of Gilgal remained as a memorial for over 2,000 years. Jerome, once known as the "patron saint of Christian and ecclesiastical learning," mentioned that the site of the camp of Gilgal and the twelve stones was still distinguishable in his day (4th century A.D.). He said it was about two miles from Jericho. By the 7th century A.D. a church had been built at the site, but the stones were said to still stand.

The name Gilgal, גִּלְגָּל , bears the number 66. As noted earlier, the triplet of 6s, 666, is the gematria for *"the head of the corner,"* referring to the topstone of the Pyramid. The number 6 in scripture also has reference to that which is in opposition to God. It is to be observed many places in the gematria of the scriptures, that the same numbers are given to seemingly opposing forces—the true and the counterfeit. In the case of Gilgal, it was a memorial to the fulfillment of God's promise to bring the Isrealites into their homeland.

In the Septuagint, the Greek text of the Old Testament, used by both Jesus and his Apostles, Gilgal is τα Γαλγαλα, which bears the number 370. The concept of "whole" in both Hebrew, שׁלם , and Greek, ὁλος , has the number equivalent of 370. It signifies completeness or perfection. In fact, the word "perfect" in Hebrew, שׁלם, is 370.

The experience of the Israelites in crossing over the Jordan and entering the promised land has been universally interpreted by all Christian peoples to be a picture of the passing of the faithful Christian through death (the Jordan) and into the heavenly home (Canaan) to become a part of the heavenly administration of the

Kingdom of God. With that concept in mind, the following demonstration of gematria is astounding:

370 Gilgal τα Γαλγαλα
370 to have power (in great power) עריץ
370 to reign מׁשל
370 perfected שׁלם
370 peace שׁלם
370 to restore שׁלם
370 whole שׁלם
370 whole ὁλος
370 to rule מׁשל
370 ruler מׁשל
370 temple οικος
370 your heavens (Psalm 8:4) שׁמיך
37   glory הכבוד
37   strength אגל

As shown on page 45, the number 37 is the prime factor in all of those multiples of 74 that pertain to Jesus Christ, God the Father, and to the Kingdom of God.

Placing the twelve stones of Gilgal in a circle would look something like this:

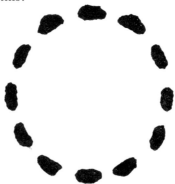

The construction of that circle would be twelve divisions of 30° each. It is interesting to note that the outer circle of stones at Stonehenge (which will be discussed later in this chapter) consisted of 30 divisions of 12° each.

THE STONES OF A CIRCLE

Each of the stones of Gilgal represented one of the tribes of Israel. They can be connected by four equilateral triangles, forming a double Star of David.

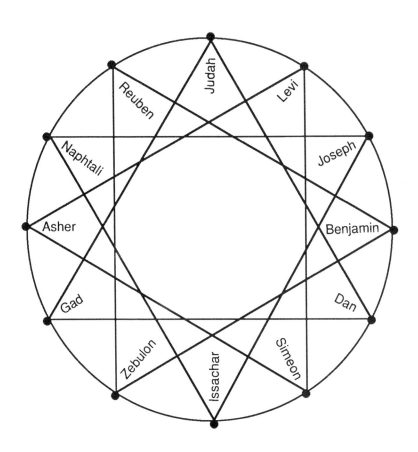

The number equivalents for the names of the 12 tribes of Israel reveal a remarkable correspndence to the completed work of redemption accomplished by the Lord Jesus Christ.

Reuben, ראובן	259	
Judah, יהודה	30	
Levi, לוי	46	
Joseph, יוסף	156	
Benjamin, בנימן	152	
Dan, דן	54	(55)
Simeon, סמצון	466	
Issachar, יששכר	830	
Zebulun, זבולן	95	
Gad, גד	7	(8)
Asher, אשר	501	
Naphtali, נפתלי	570	
	3166*	
	(3168)	

3168 Lord Jesus Christ, Κυριος Ἰησους Χριστος

3168 "For the body is not one member but many" (I Cor. 12:14)
      (Referring to faithful Christians.)
      και το σωμα ουκ εστιν εν μελος αλλα πολλα

The evidence reveals that the twelve stones of Gilgal were to be not only a memorial of the event of the Israelites crossing the Jordan and entering Canaan, but it is further a most fitting prophetic illustration of the deliverance of the faithful Christian from death and into the heavenly Kingdom.

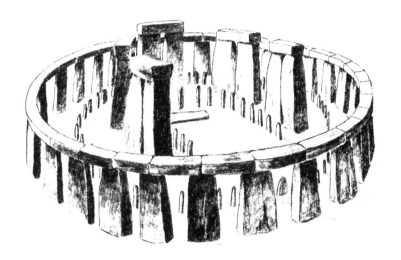

Stonehenge

The world's most well-known stone circle is of course Stonehenge—that ancient configuration of huge monoliths that has stood mute on the lonely Salisbury Plain in southern England for approximately 4,000 years.

Historians, archaeologists, astronomers, and the just plain curious have sought for centuries to solve its mysteries. Their discoveries and observations have contributed much toward the present-day knowledge of its plan and purpose, through which those lonely stones stand mute. Yet, silent as they are, if we listen, they cry out to be heard; they beg for our attention and plead for our understanding.

One cannot walk amid those old stones without experiencing the overpowering awareness of the tremendous skill, knowledge and precision of its builder. And one cannot help but wonder why was it built—what purpose did it serve?[1]

---

1 A detailed description of Stonehenge is found in *Stonehenge...a closer look,* by Bonnie Gaunt, 510 Golf Ave., Jackson, MI 49203, U.S.A., 1979 ($10.00).

THE STONES CRY OUT

Stonehenge stands lonely and forsaken in the morning mist. The Heelstone, seen through the sarsen arch 1-30 keeps its 4,000-year-old vigil over the monument.

THE STONES OF A CIRCLE

A clue to the answer can be found in its dimensions.

Stonehenge consists of several concentric circles, some of stone and some of earth. The stone circles occupy the central portion, and they are surrounded by a circle of 56 holes, which in turn is surrounded by an earth bank, which is finally surrounded by a ditch.

The outer circle of stones consisted of 30 uprights, connected at the top by 30 stone lintels. The lintels became a continuous perfect circle. This, in more modern times has been named the Sarsen Circle, because the stones are of sarsen, a kind of sandstone. The 30 uprights were placed around the circle in divisions of 12°. This circle was found to have a mean circumference of 316.8 feet.

That discovery began to change the established thinking concerning the origin and purpose of Stonehenge. As we have already noted, the figure 3168 is the gematria for Lord Jesus Christ, Κυριος Ἰησους Χριστος.

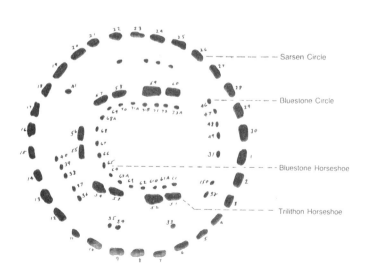

THE STONES CRY OUT

Why was the number for Lord Jesus Christ used as the measurement for that circle of stones, 2,000 years before He came to earth? What do those stones have to tell us about Jesus Christ?

Further search finds the Sarsen Circle truly remarkable. The area within that mean circumference of 316.8 feet would be 888 square yards. The gematria for Jesus, 'Ιησους, is 888. If that mean circumference were stated in yards, it would measure 29.99, and the gematria for "Thou art the Son of God," ὅτι σὺ εἶ ὁ υἱὸς τοῦ θεοῦ is 2999. If that same mean circumference were stated in megalithic yards (a unit found in the measuring of megalithic sites in England), it would be 116.4, and the title Son of God, υἱὸς θεοῦ, has a number equivalent of 1164. If a square were drawn on the outer face of the Sarsen Circle it would measure 140.8 yards, and the gematria for Saviour, σωτηρ, is 1408. The area of that square would be 1239 square yards, and the gematria for Nazarene, Ναζωραιος, is 1239. The diameter of the inner face of the Sarsen Circle is 35.8 megalithic yards, and the gematria for Messiah, משיח, is 358.

That circle of stones, standing mute for 4,000 years, cries out to be heard. It clearly relates to the Lord Jesus Christ.[1]

Immediately within the Sarsen Circle stands a circle of smaller stones, known today as the Bluestone Circle. They are of a much different geological formation than the sarsen stones. The bluestones are "eruptive rocks," known in geology as dolerite and rhyolite.

The dimensions and the geometric relationship of these two circles of stones is amazing. The relationship of the Bluestone Circle to the Sarsen Circle is identical to the relationship of the earth to a square drawn on its circumference. If the circumference of the Sarsen Circle, 316.8 feet, were redefined as a square, the Bluestone Circle would fit tangent to that square.

---

1 A comprehensive study of the relationship of Stonehenge to the Lord Jesus Christ can be found in *The Magnificent Numbers of the Great Pyramid and Stonehenge,* by Bonnie Gaunt, 510 Golf Ave., Jackson, MI 49203, U.S.A., 1985, ($10.00).

THE STONES OF A CIRCLE

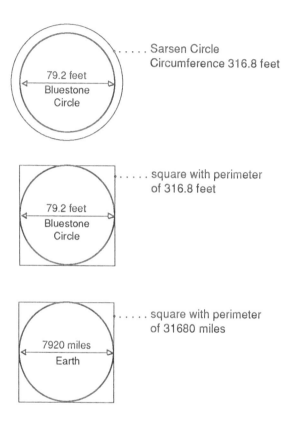

Suddenly that 4,000 year old monument takes on startling significance. It is no longer just an old pile of stones. Its architect appears to have possessed a remarkable knowledge—knowledge that we would attribute only to the Creator.

An earth diameter of 7920 miles would of course produce an earth radius of 3960 miles. This relationship is shown at Stonehenge by the relationship of the Bluestone Circle to the inmost configuration of stones, known as the Bluestone Horseshoe, which is an open-ended circle built on a diameter of 39.6 feet.

This remarkable Bluestone Horseshoe, open toward the summer sunrise, not only bears the number of the earth-radius, it can also be inscribed within the 4 equilateral triangles of the Gilgal circle of 12 stones.

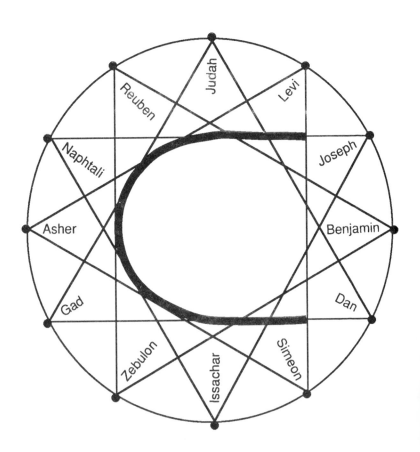

Out beyond the circles of stones is a much larger circle, known today as the Aubrey Circle, consisting of 56 holes placed equidistant around a circumference of nearly 905 feet, with an approximate 16-foot interval between their center points. The diameter of this circle of holes is 288 feet.

The Aubrey Circle diameter of 288 feet would give cause for any researcher to sit up and take notice. I ask the reader to refer to the illustration on page 18, and specifically to the projected Pythagorean right triangle, formed by the dimensions of earth and moon. The base of that triangle, planted by the Creator from the beginning, is 2880 miles. It is not by coincidence that the gematria for *"Kingdom of Heaven,"* βασιλεία τῶν οὐρανῶν is 2880. And it appears not to be a coincidence that the Aubrey Circle at Stonehenge has a diameter of 288 feet.

While 2880 is the number equivalent for *"Kingdom of Heaven,"* a square with sides of 288 has a perimeter of 1152, which is the number equivalent for *"Kingdom of God,"* τὴν βασιλείαν θεοῦ.

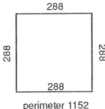

perimeter 1152

The ancient Hebrew scriptures tell a most revealing story of the first human pair, a man and a woman, made in the *"image and likeness"* of God, a human couple, made in perfection. The story reveals the tragic results of their disobedience to their Creator and their fall from that perfection. The penalty placed upon them for their disobedience was death—not immediate death, but a dying existence in which they were estranged from God.

But they were given a promise of eventual re-union with their Creator, a return to the oneness that they had originally enjoyed. The means by which this re-union could be made possible would be through a redeemer—one to pay the penalty for their disobedience and set them free from their condemnation. Such a redeemer would have to be a substitute, to take their place in death, providing them an opportunity for life. As a surety for the promise of a redeemer, God killed an animal and used its skin to clothe them.

Unto Adam also and to his wife did the Lord God make coats of skins, and clothed them. (Genesis 3:21)

How thrilling to realize that the gematria for *"coats of skins"* כתנות עור, is 288. As noted above, a square with sides of 288 has a perimeter of 1152, the number equivalent for *"Kingdom of God."*

Hidden in the transaction of providing the first human pair with coats of skins, God pointed all the way down through seven millennia to his completed kingdom in which Adam and the whole human race would be united once again with their Creator.

Stonehenge, like the Great Pyramid has now been recognized as one of the wonders that has come down to us from ancient

60

times. The prophet Jeremiah told us that God placed *"wonders"* among men to be a witness.

> *The Great, the Mighty God, the Lord of Hosts is his name . . . which hast set signs and wonders in the land of Egypt, even to this day, and in Israel, and among other men."* (Jeremiah 32:18-20)

These two ancient wonders, Stonehenge and the Great Pyramid, are indeed witnesses among men of the long-promised *"Kingdom of Heaven"* whose gematria is 2880.

The rock level base perimeter of the Great Pyramid is 288 reeds.[1]

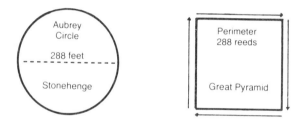

The Aubrey Circle of Stonehenge was discovered in 1666 by John Aubrey. It is a circle composed of 56 holes, 32 of which have since been covered by cement markers for purposes of observation by tourists.

In 1965, Professor Gerald S. Hawkins, an astronomer, also discovered that the Aubrey Circle, with its 56 holes, could have

---

1 The reed was the unit of measure given by God to the prophet Ezekiel (Ezekiel 40:5; 43:13). It was composed of 6 great cubits. The great cubit was 1.76 feet, thus the reed would be equivalent to 10.56 feet. Each of the lintels that were placed atop the Sarsen Circle at Stonehenge had a mean length of 10.56 feet, forming a perfect circle of 316.8 feet. The reed is thus the 30th part of the number equivalent for Lord Jesus Christ (3168).

served as a computer for the accurate prediction of eclipses.

Hawkins spent much time at Stonehenge, observing the many sighting lines, taking accurate surveys and measurements. The data he collected was then put into a computer. As he began getting analogies from the computer, Hawkins marvelled at the obvious planned precision of the whole monument. He had not been prepared for such overwhelming evidence. He found that 12 of the significant Stonehenge alignments pointed to an extreme position of the sun, and 12 alignments pointed to an extreme position of the moon.

After the computer provided Hawkins with the indisputable evidence that Stonehenge was aligned to the sun and moon, he posed the logical and inevitable question, "Why?" Why had the builders gone to all that trouble to mark the rising and setting of the sun and moon?

Hawkins, however, noted that the 56 holes of the Aubrey Circle do not mark any specific risings or settings of the sun and moon. He suggested that the circle possibly provided a protractor for the measurement of azimuth, while the bank which surrounds it provided an artificial horizon.

Evidence has since shown that it can indeed serve as a protractor for the measurement of azimuth.

On the authority of Hawkins' suggestion, I tried something. The chronology of the Bible is based on a cycle of 7,000 years. Realizing that a circle represents eternity, having no beginning nor ending, and that one circuit of its circumference would thus be a finite measure—a specific period of time—I wondered if this finite measure of time could be the 7,000 years pertaining to man's history. Thus when viewing the 56 holes of the Aubrey Circle as a protractor for the measurement of azimuth, it becomes a "time line," like the numbers around the face of a clock. How interesting to note that the number equivalent for *"everlasting"* יום is 56, and for *"time"* יום is also 56. The gematria is telling us that this is a circle of time.

When this hypothesis was tried, it was found that all of the sun

---

1 Gerald S. Hawkins, *Stonehenge Decoded*, Dell Publishing Co., New York, p. 107.

and moon alignments which Hawkins proved accurate on the computer, also crossed the protractor, or "time line" at important dates in recorded Biblical and secular history regarding man's relationship with his Creator. The evidence was overwhelming; those stones with their sighting alignments were placed in their strategic positions by someone with a knowledge of the future, for they pointed exactly to events which were not to take place for hundreds, even thousands of years! Those events are now well-established facts of history.[1]

These 56 holes which outline the circumference of the Aubrey Circle, like the face of a giant chronometer, fix in time the significant events in man's relationship to God. How fitting that the Psalmist, David, over and over again, exclaimed *"Blessed be Jehovah my rock,"* צוּרִי יְהוָה בָּרוּךְ which has a number equivalent of 560; and those of mankind who enjoy this special relationship with God are called *"Saints of the Most High,"* קַדִּישֵׁי עֶלְיוֹנִין, which is, by gematria, also 560.

For the person standing at the point of center in the Aubrey Circle, the distance to any point on the circle is 144 feet, the square of the foundation number. As all students of the Book of Revelation know, 144,000 is the number of those who stand with the Lamb of God on Mount Zion.

Surely the Architect of Stonehenge had an intimate knowledge of the universe and of prophetic scripture.

Hawkins, after his valuable research at Stonehenge, came to a positive conclusion: the primary alignment, which forms the axis of the monument, marks the sunrise at the summer solstice.[2] A conclusion shared by most researchers and archaeologists who have studied Stonehenge. This alignment of the axis did not, however, pass through the center of the Aubrey Circle, therefore its center is not the true center of the monument. The axis in fact passes through the center of the Sarsen Circle—that circle of giant

---

1 A detailed description of these alignments and their prophetic impact can be found in *Stonehenge...a closer look,* by Bonnie Gaunt, 510 Golf Avenue, Jackson, MI 49203, U.S.A. ($10,00).

2 Gerald S. Hawkins, *Stonehenge Decoded,* Del Publications, New York, 1965, p. 136.

monoliths whose mean diameter bears the same number as the Lord Jesus Christ:

316.8 feet - mean circumference of Sarsen Circle
3168 - Lord Jesus Christ Κυριος Ιησους Χριστος

On the morning of the summer solstice, the longest day of the year, when the sun rises at its most northerly extreme, the person standing in the exact center of the Sarsen Circle would see the first appearance of the sun slightly to the left (north) of the Heel Stone—a huge unhewn stone standing at a distance of 256 feet. As the sun rises it appears to move to the right (south) and momentarily disappears behind the top of the Heel Stone. Then it suddenly emerges as a golden crown atop that ancient stone. This beautiful sight could be seen 4,000 years ago, and it can still be seen today.

Because of a phenomenon known as the precession of the equinoxes, the sun moves back slightly along the ecliptic, making the point of sunrise move gradually to the right, or south. This great cycle of the precession of the equinoxes, caused by the wobble of the earth's axis, requires about 26,000 years for a complete revolution.

From the time of the construction of Stonehenge to today, the sun at the solstice has not separated from the Heelstone. Through 4,000 years, the sun still crowns that ancient stone with its golden glow. And although the relative position of the sun appears to move, the permanent position of the Heelstone becomes a fixed marker for the azimuth of sunrise, unchangeable through time.

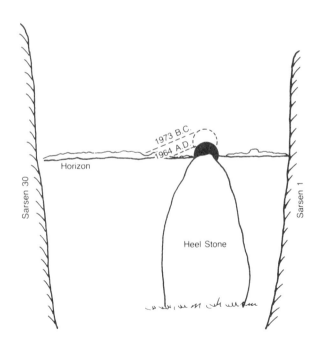

Once again we stand in awe of the infinite knowledge and foresight of the builder! What man could have invented a devise that would permanently fix the azimuth of sunrise? Yet, the builder of Stonehenge did it with a rough unhewn stone! The angle from north, is 51^0 51 '.

Once again I refer the reader to the illustration on page 18. The earth-commensurate pyramid, constructed on the centers of the earth and moon, has a base angle of 51^0 51 '—the precise proportions of the Great Pyramid in Egypt.

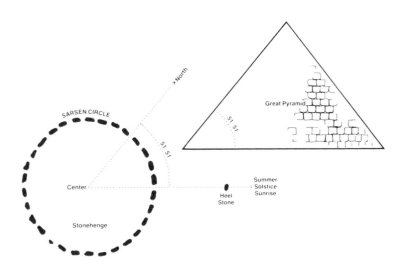

It was no coincidence that the Great Pyramid was built on the dimensions of earth and moon, and it is also no coincidence that its base angle of 51^0 51 ' is also the fundamental orientation of Stonehenge.

Did the Architect of the Great Pyramid know the earth-moon relationship? Did he also know the azimuth of summer solstice sunrise on the lonely desolate island we now call England? The builder of Stonehenge could not have merely copied this angle from the Great Pyramid, since both the solstice sunrise and the direction of north are not man-maneuverable, but were placed there by the Creator.

After 4,000 years, the stones of these two monuments continue to cry out. They tell us of an intelligent Creator, of one who knew history in advance, one who planned and provided for man's redemption through the Lord Jesus Christ.

The Coronation Chair in Westminster Abbey, was built for Edward I in A.D. 1296. The Coronation Stone resides beneath the seat. Every British monarch since Edward I has received their coronation while seated in this chair.

4

A STONE OF DESTINY

Among the stones that have come down to us from the ancient world is a small unpretentious block of sandstone about 26 " in length, 16 " wide and 10½ " high, weighing a little over 300 pounds. The stone attracts little attention, and rests, unknown to most of the world, under a chair in Westminster Abbey.

The chair was built specifically to hold the stone. It is called St. Edward's Chair, or the Coronation Chair.

In the year A.D. 1953, Queen Elizabeth II was crowned, sitting in the chair, upon the stone. In fact, every monarch who has ruled in England since James I have received their coronation while seated upon this stone. Why?

What does this little block of greyish sandstone have to do with royalty? From whence did the stone come to Westminster Abbey?

This Coronation Stone came to London in the year A.D. 1296, when it was given to Edward I by the Scots for safe-keeping. Recognizing the importance of this ancient stone, Edward I had a beautiful hardwood chair constructed, into which it was placed. The chair was then placed in Westminster Abbey, where it remains to this day.

Dean Stanley, in his *Memorials of Westminster Abbey,* said: "The chief object of attraction to this day, to the innumerable visitors to the Abbey, is probably that ancient Irish monument of the empire known as the Coronation Stone." He went on to say that "It is the one primeval monument which binds together the whole empire."

THE STONES CRY OUT

The stone has been held in such reverence that even when the treaty of Northampton in 1328 allowed the emeralds, pearls, and rubies of the empire to be carried away, they would not suffer the stone to be removed.

Yet, in the darkness of the early hours of Christmas morning, in 1950, while Britain lay sleeping, the stone was stealthily removed from the chair, dragged across the carpeted altar steps, and out of the Abbey. This crime of sacrilege shocked all of Britain.

Within a week it was known that the Coronation Stone had been taken to Scotland, and a letter of petition was received by King George VI stating that the stone was the "most ancient symbol of Scottish nationality . . . and its proper place of retention is among his Majesty's Scottish people, who, above all, hold this symbol dear . . ."

The petitioner requested that the stone reside in Scotland.

The stone was subsequently wrapped in a Scottish flag and left upon the high altar of the Abbey of Arbroath in Scotland, and the British were notified of where it could be found.

It is said that the removing of the stone from Westminster Abbey resulted in the cracking of it into two pieces. And it is claimed that a copy of the Scottish Declaration of Independence was placed between the halves, and the two pieces of the stone sealed by doweling and cement.

Why did the Scottish Nationalists treasure this tradition so highly that they were willing to risk the theft of it from Westminster Abbey? It is because prior to its having been given to Edward I in 1296, the stone had been the possession of the kings of Scotland.

The Coronation Stone came to Scotland in the year A.D. 513, at the request of Fergus the great. Fergus, from the Irish kingdom of Dalriada, had invaded the land of the Picts, on the western coasts of Scotland and there set up his kingdom. But to give his coronation the proper symbol of authority, he sent word to his brother, Muircheartach, who was then king of Ireland, to transport the stone to Scotland for the occasion. Fergus was crowned king of Scotland upon the stone in the fortress of Dunadd in the year A.D. 513, and there the stone remained for 62 years.

A STONE OF DESTINY

In the year A.D. 575 the grandson of Fergus removed the stone to Iona, and there Aidan, a son of the king of Dalriada (Ireland) was crowned upon it.

Thus, according to Scottish history, the stone had come from Ireland. It was the Coronation Stone upon which the Irish monarchs were crowned. The Irish called it Lea-Fail, which meant "stone of fate," or "stone of destiny." According to Irish history it had been in their possession, and they had crowned their kings upon it for well over 1,000 years. But where did the Irish kings get the stone—their Lea-Fail?

It is of interest to note a few references to the Lea-Fail, or Stone of Destiny from the Encyclopedia Britannica, edition 1961:

> (Book No. 23, page 540) The coronation chair, which stands in the Confessor's chapel, dates from the time of Edward I and contains beneath its seat the stone of Scone, on which the Scottish kings were crowned. The stone is of Scottish origin, but tradition identifies it with Jacob's pillow at Bethel.

> (Book No. 16, page 790) The inauguration stone of the Irish kings, the Lea-Fail, or Stone of Destiny, fabled to have been the pillow of the patriarch Jacob when he dreamed of the heavenly ladder, was said to have been presented by Murkertagh to the king of Dalriada, by whom it was conveyed to Dunstaffnage castle in Scotland.

> (Book No. 12, page 359) Inisfail, a poetic name for Ireland. It is derived from *inis* "island" and *Lea-fail,* the celebrated stone identified in Irish legend with the stone on which the patriarch Jacob slept when he dreamed of the heavenly ladder.

Tradition usually has some basis or foundation for its existence. But do we have any evidence in support of this ancient tradition that the stone Lea-Fail was the stone that Jacob used for a pillow?

An analysis of the structure of the stone could determine its origin, if similar rock could be found. Such tests have been made, and to date, no rock formation of its kind has been found in England, Scotland or Ireland. However, on the suggestion of the

71

tradition that this stone came from the place called Bethel, a similar search has been made in that locality. It was no surprise to find there a rock of identical geological structure. A microscopic test of the rock found at modern-day Bethel, matched perfectly with the same test made of the Coronation Stone. But how did it get from Bethel to Ireland?

Janet and Colin Bord in *Mysterious Britain,* (Granada Publishing Limited, London, 1983), have capsulized the travels of the stone thus:

> ...no one knows for certain where this stone originated nor why it has always had so much significance as a stone of inauguration. Traditionally it was the pillow used by Jacob when he had his dream of the angels at Bethel. Later it was in the Temple of Jerusalem and the kings of Judah were crowned upon it. Then in the fourth century B.C., the daughter of the last king of Judah and the prophet Jeremiah travelled through Egypt and Spain to Ireland, taking the stone with them. The princess from Judah married into the royal line of the Irish kings, and for centuries afterward the kings of Ireland were crowned above the stone.
>
> Some versions say that it came to Scotland in A.D. 500, others say the date was about A.D. 900, but it was at a time when the Picts were defeated and one of the royal house of Ireland was crowned king of a united Scotland. The stone was kept at Scone where thirty-four successive Scottish kings were crowned sitting above it. In 1297 Edward I took the stone to London and had it placed beneath his newly-made Coronation Chair in Westminster Abbey. It remained there until 1950 when Scottish Nationalists removed it one night and took it into hiding in Scotland. In 1951 it was recovered and restored to the Abbey.

On June 28, 1837, on the occasion of the coronation of Queen Victoria, the London *Sun* published the following description of the coronation chair and its stone:

> This chair, commonly called St. Edward's chair, is an ancient seat of solid hardwood, with back and sides of the same,

variously painted, in which the kings of Scotland were in former periods constantly crowned, but, having been brought out of the kingdom by Edward I, in the year 1296, after he had totally overcome John Baliol, king of Scots, it has ever since remained in the Abbey of Westminster, and has been the chair in which the succeeding kings and queens of this realm have been inaugurated. It is in height six feet and seven inches, in breadth at the bottom thirty-eight inches, and in depth twenty-four inches; from the seat to the bottom is twenty-five inches; the breadth of the seat within the sides is twenty-eight inches, and the depth eighteen inches. At nine inches from the ground is a board, supported at the four corners by as many lions. Between the seat and this board is enclosed a stone, commonly called Jacob's or the fatal Marble, Stone, which is an oblong of about twenty-two inches in length, thirteen inches broad and eleven inches deep; of a steel color, mixed with some veins of red. History relates that it is the stone whereon the patriarch Jacob laid his head in the plains of Luz . . . . This stone was conveyed into Ireland by way of Spain about 700 years before Christ.

The author of the article was somewhat inaccurate in his chronology, but the travels of the stone are supported by other historians. Spain was once Iberia (a derivative of "Hebrew" or "Heber") and when the Iberians came to Ireland, they gave their name to the island, calling it "Iberne," later called "Hibernia."

There is evidence from the Old Testament that the Hebrew people had a coronation stone upon which the king stood (or sat) to claim his right of rulership.

In the second book of Kings is recorded the story of the usurpation of the throne of Judah by Athaliah, the mother of king Ahaziah. Upon the death of Ahaziah, she attempted the assassination of all the king's children and then claimed the right to the throne for herself. She seemingly succeeded. And for seven years she ruled the nation of Judah.

Unknown to Athaliah, a sister of Ahaziah, named Jehosheba, had stolen the youngest of the king's sons, a tiny baby, and hid him. This rightful heir to the throne of Judah was Joash. He was successfully hidden for over six years.

In the seventh year there was a rebellion against Athaliah; and the priest, accompanied by the military captains of Judah, brought the boy Joash out of hiding. They brought him to the temple, and as Joash stood upon the coronation stone, they placed the royal crown upon his head, clapped their hands and shouted, *"God save the king."*

And when Athaliah heard the noise of the guard and of the people, she came to the people into the temple of the Lord. And when she looked, behold the king stood by (upon) a pillar, as the manner was, and the princes and the trumpeters by the king, and all the people rejoiced, and blew with trumpets. And Athaliah rent her clothes, and cried 'Treason, Treason.' " (II Kings 11:14)

The Hebrew scholar, Isaac Leeser, in his translation of the Old Testament, renders the preposition *"upon"* rather than *"by."* The boy Joash was standing upon the pillar. Leeser goes on to say that this ritual was *"according to custom."*

When Athaliah saw Joash standing on the coronation stone, she knew that he had been proclaimed king. She attempted to flee for her life, but the captains and the officers took her to the horses' stall, and slew her.

The fact of the king standing upon the pillar denoted the right to the power of rulership. It is interesting to note that the statement *"and behold the king stood upon the pillar,"* has a number equivalent of 500; likewise ruler, שׂר , is 500, prince, שׂר , is 500, and power, δυναμιν , is the triplet of fives, 555.

This pillar, which in Hebrew is *Matstebah*, מַצֵּבָת , bears the number 137. To show the power represented by this pillar stone, draw a circle with a circumference of 137; draw a square tangent to the circle, then change the square to a circle of the same perimeter, and the diamater of that larger circle will be 55.5 (power).

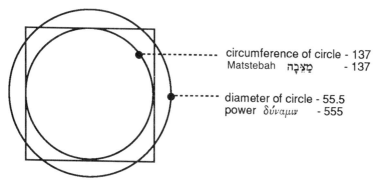

circumference of circle - 137
Matstebah מַצֵבָה - 137

diameter of circle - 55.5
power δύναμιν - 555

Thus the biblical record does indeed reveal that the Hebrew people had a coronation stone. But where did it come from?

Since all the tradition and all the history of the Stone of Destiny tells of its origin with Jacob let's turn again to the biblical record.

And Jacob went out from Beersheba, and went toward Haran. And he lighted upon a certain place, and tarried there all night, because the sun was set; and he took of the stones of that place, and put them for his pillows, and lay down in that place to sleep.

And he dreamed, and behold a ladder was set up on the earth, and the top of it reached to heaven: and behold the angels of God ascending and descending upon it. And behold, the Lord stood above it, and said, 'I am the Lord God of Abraham thy father, and the God of Isaac: the land whereon thou liest, to thee will I give it, and to thy seed; and thy seed shall be as the dust of the earth, and thou shalt spread abroad to the west, and to the east, and to the north and to the south: and in thee and in thy seed shall all the families of the earth be blessed. And, behold, I am with thee, and will keep thee in all places whither thou goest, and will bring thee again into this land; for I will not leave thee, until I have done that which I have spoken to the of.'

And Jacob rose up early in the morning, and took the stone that he had put for his pillows, and set it up for a pillar, and poured oil upon the top of it. And he called the name of the place Bethel: but the name of that city was called Luz at the first.

And Jacob vowed a vow, saying, 'If God will be with me, and will keep me in this way that I go, and will give me bread to eat, and raiment to put on, so that I come again to my father's house in peace; then shall the Lord be my God: and this stone, which I have set for a pillar, shall be God's house: and of all that thou shalt give me I will surely give the tenth unto thee.'

Jacob realized that what he had just experienced was more than merely a dream. He had been the recipient of the promise that had first been given to his grandfather, Abraham, and had been repeated to his father, Isaac—the promise from God that through his seed, or posterity a blessing would be given to *"all the families of the earth."*

Jacob had been profoundly touched! His response came from the utmost depth of his being. He took the stone on which his head had rested, and set it up as a *memorial.* It is the Hebrew word *Matstsebah,* the same word as used in Isaiah 19:19-20 describing the Great Pyramid. He anointed it with oil and called it Bethel, which means *"the house of God."*

The statement that Jacob made that morning—*"and the stone shall become the house of God"*—were not idle words; however, Jacob was probably not aware of their profound significance. That statement, by its gematria, points all the way down throug time to the one through whom that promised blessing would com *"And the stone shall become the house of God,"* אלהים

והאבן יהיה בית , has a number equivalent of 592. /
with sides of 592 has a perimeter of 2368, which is the ε
for Jesus Christ.

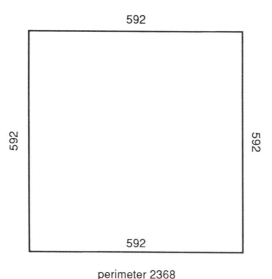

592

592   592

592

perimeter 2368

592 - "and the stone shall become the house of God"

והאבן יהיה בית אלהים

2368 - Jesus Christ, Ἰησους Χριστος

Whether Jacob took the stone with him at that time, or twenty years later when he returned to that place, the record is not clear. That it was in Jacob's possession is recorded in Genesis 49:24. Jacob, when conferring a blessing on each of his twelve sons, gave a special and significant blessing to Joseph, that he would be the one to possess *"the Shepherd, the stone of Israel."*

That the stone was given this name is evidence of its importance to Jacob. He had first named it Bethel, *"the house of God,"* and now he calls it *"the Shepherd, the stone of Israel."* His recognition of God as his Shepherd is evident. The stone was the symbol of the covenant that God had made with him.

The gematria of that name is further evidence of its place in a grand design. The Shepherd, רעה , bears the number equivalent of 275. A square with sides of 275 has a perimeter of 1100.

THE STONES CRY OUT

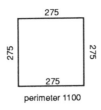

perimeter 1100

The number 1100 points all the way down to earth's rightful ruler: he is the *foundation,* סוֹפָד , 110, of all the works of God; he is the one who possesses *excelling greatness,* ὑπερβάλλον μέγεθος 1100; the *stone,* λίθινα, 110, the one represented by the gold-covered topstone of the Great Pyramid (gold, דָּהָב , 11) is the one whose name is *Wonderful,* פֶּלֶא , 111, the one who was the *Root of Jesse,* יְשַׁי שֶׁי , 1110.

Further evidence of the importance of the Shepherd Stone is in the relationship of its gematria to our solar system. *The Shepherd,* רֹעֶה , has the number equivalent of 275. If 275 were the diameter of a circle, the circumference of that circle would be 864 (the solar number—the diameter of the sun is 864,000 miles). If that same circle were changed to a square, keeping the same perimeter, each side would be 216, which is the lunar number (the diameter of the moon is 2160 miles).

As shown in the earth-moon model on page 18, these numbers bear a direct relationship to earth's rightful ruler.

2160 (miles) diameter of moon
2160 Kingdom of the Father, βασιλεία τῶν πατρός
216 power נְבוּרָה

864,000 (miles) diameter of sun
864 He shall reign (Rev. 11:15) βασιλεύσει
864 Holy of Holies αγιων
864 life ζωην

Through gematria it becomes evident that this stone—the Bethel Stone, later called the Shepherd Stone—points down through time to the one to come whose right it is to rule—the one through whom the blessing of life will come to *"all the families of the earth"*— Jesus Christ.

A STONE OF DESTINY

The next mention of this stone in the Old Testament was many years later when the Hebrew people had fled from the land of Egypt and were thirsting for water in the Sinai desert. Moses, their leader, was instructed to smite *"the rock"* and water would come out, so that the people and all the cattle could drink. The first mention of obtaining water from the rock may give the appearance that it was a rock native to the area, and perhaps permanently a part of the terrain. However, many years later, Moses was again told to obtain water from the rock, and in this account of the incident, it becomes apparent that the rock was familiar to them.

> *And the Lord spake unto Moses, saying: 'Take the rod, and gather the assembly together, and speak ye unto the rock before their eyes; and it shall give forth his water, and thou shalt bring forth to them water out of the rock.... And Moses and Aaron gathered the congregation together before the rock..., and Moses lifted up his hand, and with his rod he smote the rock twice; and the water came out abundantly, and the congregation drank and their beasts also."* (Numbers 20:5-11)

It must be realized that the Hebrew people had moved no less than twenty-one times since the first incident of obtaining water from the rock, and were now in a location in a far different part of Sinai. Yet Moses was told to *"gather the congregation together before the rock."* They did not need to be told which rock; the term *"the rock"* was sufficient because they already knew that the rock they carried with them could supply water.

It may be difficult for us today to picture water coming out of such a small rock, especially the quantity that would be needed to quench the thirst of more than two million people plus their cattle and other livestock. However, when this event was recalled by King David more than 500 years later, he spoke of water enough to fill a river:

> *He brought streams also out of the rock, and caused waters to run down like rivers."* (Psalm 78:16)

> *Behold he smote the rock, that the waters gushed out, and*

79

the streams overflowed.'' (Psalm 78:20)

He opened the rock, and the waters gushed out; they ran in the dry places like a river.'' (Psalm 105:41)

About 500 more years after King David's time, the prophet Isaiah spoke of the same event:

He caused the waters to flow out of the rock for them: he clave the rock also, and the waters gushed out. (Isaiah 48:21)

That they carried the rock with them was confirmed by the Apostle Paul. He mentioned the incident of water flowing from the rock, and his language makes it clear that the rock was part of their possessions which they carried with them on their journey through the desert. He said:

And all did drink the same spiritual drink; for they drank of that spiritual Rock that followed them: and that Rock was Christ.''

The word *followed* is from the Greek, ἀκολουθέω, which literally means to carry along with or to accompany.

Paul not only settled the matter that the rock was portable, and went with them, he also informed us of its symbolism—it represented Christ. Why? Because it was the means of salvation to the Hebrew people in the desert. It literally saved them from dying of thirst. Thus it follows logically that the gematria for Saviour, מושיע, is 426, and the gematria for *"water out of the rock,''* ומים נסלע, is also 426, showing that the rock was indeed a symbol of the Saviour.

Further evidence that the Bethel Stone and the rock from which water flowed were one and the same can also be obtained from the gematria. The number value for *"water from the rock,''* וּמַיִם מִסֶּלַע , (Nehemiah 9:15) is 296. The gematria for Son of Man, ο υιος ανθρωπου, is 2960, for Only Begotten, μονογενη, is 296, and for *"eternal salvation,''* σωτηριας αιωνιου is 2960. Thus water from the rock is in perfect harmony with that of which it is indeed a symbol. The relationship of this to the Bethel Stone can best be shown by the following simple figure:

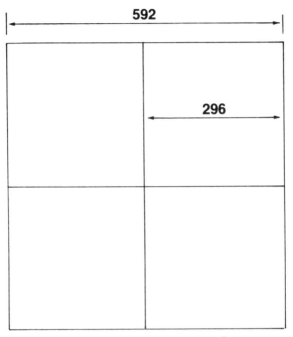

One side of small square, 296 — "water from the rock, ‎ונים מסלע‎, 296
One side of large square, 592 — "the stone shall become the house of God,
‎והאבן יהיה בית אלהים‎, 592
Perimeter of large square, 2368 — Jesus Christ, $'I\eta\sigma o\upsilon\varsigma\ X\rho\iota\sigma\tau o\varsigma$, 2368

The harmony of this numerical relationship bears testimony that they are parts of a whole—a complete concept. It can also be shown by the geometric principle of the circle and the square of same perimeter as in the example below.

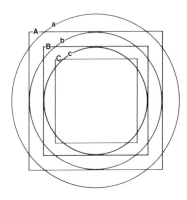

The gematria for Jesus Christ is 2368, therefore let us use that figure as the number of units in the circumference of Circle *a*. Starting with this dimension, by simple mathematics the dimensions of the other circles and squares can be obtained. In doing this the beautiful numbers begin to appear: numbers relating to the Bethel Stone, to the rock from which Moses obtained water, to Jesus Christ, and to the place of his death, Golgotha. The numbers are telling the story of the confirming of the covenant to Jacob that *"all the families of the earth"* would be blessed; the means of that blessing would be through the Lord Jesus Christ, as was pictured by the life-preserving water that flowed from the rock.

236.8 - Square A and Circle a
2368 - Jesus Christ, Ἰησους Χριστος

186.0 - Square B and Circle b
186 - Great Rock, סלע כבד (Isaiah 32:2)
186 - Golgotha, Γολγοθα

146.0 - Square C and Circle c
146 - Jehovah-nissee, יהוה נסי (Exodus 17:15)
1460 - *a precious cornerstone, a sure foundation,*
פנת יקרת מוסד מוס ד (Isaiah 28:16)

59.2 - one side of Square A
59.2 - diameter of Circle B
592 - *and the stone shall become the house of God,*
   ‎והאבן יהיה בית אלהים (Genesis 28:22, The Bethel stone)

29.6 - radius of Circle b
296 - *water from the rock,* ‎ומים מסלע (Nehemiah 9:6)
296 - rock, ‎צור
2960 - eternal salvation, σωτηριας αιωνιου (Hebrews 5:9)
2960 - Son of Man, ο υιος ανθρωπου
296 - Only Begotten, μονογενη

301 - *He is the rock,* ‎הצור (Deut. 32:4)
301 - Calvary, κρανιον

The relationship of Circle *b* to Circle *a* in the above diagram is precisely the relationship of the Sarsen Circle to the Bluestone Circle at Stonehenge. A fact that is beyond the reach of coincidence.

Using the same figure as above, if we were to superimpose a pyramid whose base were the diameter of Circle *c,* and the apex reached to Square *A*, its base angle would be precisely 51° 51 ″—the same exact angle of base to apex of the Great Pyramid.

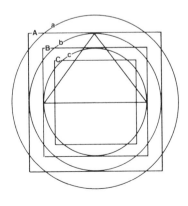

Just as the topstone of the Great Pyramid has been shown to represent Jesus Christ, so the apex of the above pyramid reaches to Square *A* whose perimeter bears the number of Jesus Christ, 2368.

Using the same diagram, the earth-moon model shown on page 18 can be overlaid with precision.

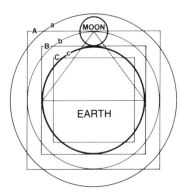

Surely the Architect of those orbs was building one great harmonious design—a design that tells the story of the redemption of man through Jesus Christ, and his eventual oneness with his Creator in the promised Kingdom of God.

The record has been written in stone, and those stones indeed cry out.

The Stone of Destiny, residing quietly from the world, beneath the seat of England's coronation chair, has a time-worn groove across the middle of its top, and two metal rings, one at each end. Obviously it once held a stave through its metal rings by which it could be carried. The time-worn groove is evidence of many years of having been carried in this manner.

Just as the Israelites, moving from place to place in the desert of Sinai, carried the revered Ark of the Covenant by means of staves, so the revered stone, the Bethel Stone, the Shepherd, the Rock of Israel, was carried on the shoulders of men.

5

Stones for a Foundation

The discussion of the building blocks of creation in chapter 1 cries out for a broader examination of the concept of foundations.

In the Old Testament, the book of Job contains some profound questions relating to earth-science and the beginning of things. God asked Job:

Where wast thou when I laid the foundations of the earth? Declare if thou hast understanding. Who laid the measures thereof, if thou knowest? Or who hath stretched the line upon it? Whereupon are the foundations thereof fastened? Or who laid the cornerstone thereof? (Job 38:6)

The Hebrew scholar, Isaac Leeser, translates the Hebrew text more precisely by:

Upon what are her foundation-pillars made to sink? Or who laid the cornerstone?

Does the earth have foundation-pillars? Does the earth have a cornerstone?

It sounds more like a description of the Great Pyramid. Perhaps the simile was intended. The Great Pyramid does indeed have foundation-pillars that are sunk beneath its four base corners; and it does have a magnificent cornerstone—a topstone that has never been placed upon its summit platform.

The gematria for the statement in Job suggests that the foundation-pillars and the cornerstone relate to the Creator and the work of creation through the Son. *"I laid the foundation of the earth,"* ארץ has a number equivalent of 291. The four foundation-pillars would be 4 × 291 or 1164. It is not by coincidence that the gematria for Son of God, $\upsilon\iota o\varsigma\,\Theta\epsilon o\upsilon$ is 1164.

It is also in complete harmony with the statement in Psalm 102:25 *"Thou hast laid the foundation of the earth,"* הָאָרֶץ יָסַדְתָּ 740. And as shown on page 5, the foundation number, 12, when multiplied by 74 produces 888 which is the gematria for Jesus.

The scripture in Job goes on to say, *"or who hath laid the cornerstone thereof,"* אִי מִי־יָרָה אֶבֶן פִּנָּתָהּ and has a number value of 860. The title "God" in Hebrew, אֱלֹהִים , is 86, which is the sum of 12 + 74. How beautiful to realize that *"The majesty of Jehovah"* (Isaiah 24:14), גְּאוֹן יְהוָה , also bears the number 86.

"In the beginning God, (Elohim, 86) created the heavens and the earth." "The majesty of Jehovah," גְּאוֹן יְהוָה , 86, is wondrously displayed in all *"his works,"* פָּעֳלוֹ , 186. In Isaiah 32:2 he is called *"Great Rock,"* כֶּבֶד סֶלַע , 186.

When the Psalmist, David, declared *"Jehovah is my Rock,"* (Psalm 18:2) he was speaking of the great foundation of all creation. The statement in Hebrew is סַלְעִי יְהוָה and bears the number 186.

As shown on page 9, the literal bedrock foundation of the earth is composed of 12 elements, and the sum of their atomic weight is 186.

If the four foundation-pillars of the earth were multiplied by 186 the product would be 744 (4 × 186 = 744). The concept could be shown graphically by a square with sides of 186, giving a perimeter of 744.

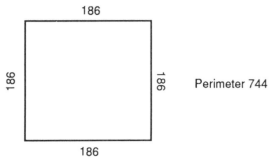

Simply re-define the square as a circle of the same circumference and the diameter of the circle would be 236.8. The gematria for Jesus Christ, 'Ιησους Χριστος is 2368.

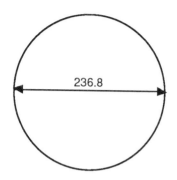

Circumference 744
"laid the foundation of the house (of God)"
(Ezra 5:16) יְהַב אשׁ דִּי־בַית 744
Diameter 236.8
Jesus Christ, Ιησους Χριστος, 2368

Draw a square tangent to the above circle and the perimeter would be 947. Re-define that square as a circle of the same circumference and the diameter of the new circle will be 301.

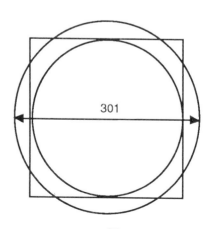

THE STONES CRY OUT

What does the figure 301 have to do with the concept of a rock and a foundation?

Before attempting to answer that, let's look at the figure 186 as defining the circumference of a circle, rather than one side of a square as in the above demonstration. A circumference of 186 will have a diameter of 59.2. It is the number that relates to the memorial-stone that Jacob set up as a pillar and said *"The stone shall become the house of God,"* והאבן יהיה בית אלהים, 592.

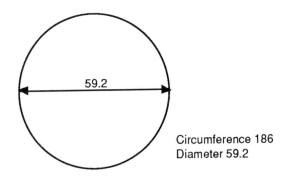

Circumference 186
Diameter 59.2

When we draw a square tangent to the above circle, the perimeter will be 236.8, which is the gematria for Jesus Christ.

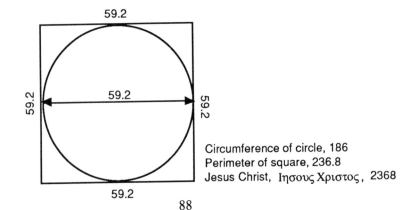

Circumference of circle, 186
Perimeter of square, 236.8
Jesus Christ, Ιησους Χριστος, 2368

88

If we were to re-define the above square as a circle of the same circumference, and draw a square tangent to that circle, the perimeter of the larger square would be 301. Why 301?

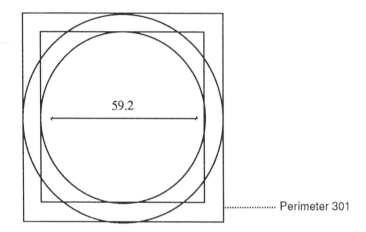

59.2

.... Perimeter 301

The Song of Moses, as recorded in the book of Deuteronomy is a beautiful hymn to the universe, praising the majesty of Jehovah. It reads, in part:

Give ear, O ye heavens, and I will speak; and hear, O earth, the words of my mouth...I will publish the name of the Lord: ascribe ye greatness unto our God. He is the Rock, his work is perfect; for all his ways are judgment: a God of truth and without iniquity, just and right is he... (Deut. 32:1-4)

Moses described him as a great foundation Rock— *"He is the Rock,"* הצור who bears the number 301.

There is another rock that bears this number—a rock that has been the place of union between God and man down through the centuries of time. It was the rocky summit of Mount Moriah, where Abraham offered his son in sacrifice—a picture of an event that was to take place on that same rock more than two thousand years after, when God gave his son in sacrifice.

Long after the time of Abraham, one of his descendants, King David, purchased this rock from a man named Ornan. David talked with a heavenly messenger who was standing on the Rock, and afterward was impelled to offer there, a sacrifice of thanksgiving.

Later, David's son, Solomon, built a temple there. After the temple was burned by Nebuchadnezzar in 586 B.C., the Rock lay desolate until the return of the three tribes, Judah, Benjamin and Levi, from their Babylonian exile, when, under the leadership of Zerubbabel, another temple was built upon it.

In 21 B.C., Herod the Great, who ruled the land of Judea under Caesar Augustus of Rome, built a third temple on the ruins of the second temple. This beautiful and imposing edifice was destroyed by the army of Titus in A.D. 70—Rome's seige of Jerusalem. The only thing that remained was a portion of a retaining wall, now known as the Wailing Wall, or Western Wall.

In A.D. 637 the Caliph Omar built a temporary structure upon the Rock, to be followed in A.D. 738 by the beautiful Mosque of Omar, better known as the Dome of the Rock. The floor of the inner chamber of this mosque is the Rock.

The Rock was, in fact, the foundation for each of the structures that had been built upon it. This Rock that is sacred to Arab, Jew, and Christian, is also known as the Foundation, which in Hebrew is אש , 301, and sometimes simply as the Rock, הצור , which also has a number equivalent of 301.

When King David desired the Rock for a place of sacrifice, he purchased it from a man named Ornan, אָרְנָן , whose gematria is 301.

In A.D. 33, upon this Rock, Jesus, the world's Saviour was crucified. The place of the crucifixion was then called Calvary, $\kappa\rho\alpha\nu\iota\nu$, which bears the number 301.

A square with sides of 301 has a perimeter of 1204, which is the gematria for *"The Holy Mount at Jerusalem,"* (Isaiah 27:13), בדר הקדש בירושלם .

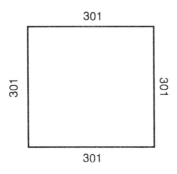

Each side, 301 — Calvary, κρανιον, 301
Perimeter, 1204 — The Holy Mount at Jerusalem,
בדר הקדש בירושלם,1204

This great foundation Rock bears a remarkable relationship to the topstone of the Great Pyramid by its geometry and its gematria.

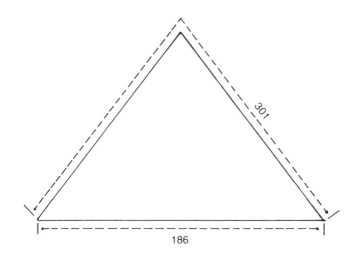

If the topstone were assigned a base of 186 units, the combined sides would be 301 units. How appropriate that the other name for Calvary is Golgotha, $\Gamma o\lambda\gamma o\theta\alpha$, which has the number equivalent of 186.

86   God אלהים

86   The Majesty of Jehovah (Isaiah 24:14) גאון יהוה

86   Galilee $\Gamma a\lambda\iota\lambda a\iota a$

860   "who hath laid the cornerstone thereof" (Job 38:6)

186   Jehovah is my Rock (Psalm 18:2) יהוה סלעי

186   His work (Deuteronomy 32:4) פעלו

186   Great Rock (Isaiah 32:2) סלע כבד

186   Golgotha $\Gamma o\lambda\gamma o\theta\alpha$

301   He is the Rock (Deuteronomy 32:4) הצור

301   Foundation (Ezra 5:16) אש

301   Ornan (one time owner of the Rock) ארנן

301   The Rock (Psalm 114:8) הצור

301   Calvary $\kappa\rho\alpha\nu\iota o\nu$

Down through the centuries of time this meeting place between God and man has borne the number 301. A common thread ties together the history of this sacred spot. An ancient Hebrew legend even suggests that this rock, that they called *Eben Shetiyyah,* the Stone of Foundation, "was the first solid thing created, and was placed by God amidst the as yet boundless fluid of primeval waters...so God built the earth concentrically around this stone." Legends generally have some basis for their existence. When God asked Job, *"Where wast thou when I laid the foundations of the earth?"* he was undoubtedly talking about the very foundation of Creation—*"Jehovah is my Rock,"* (Psalm 18:2), 186, as represented by the rock, Golgotha, 186.

The Apostle Paul included the Lord Jesus Christ in this foundation concept when he said:

> *Other foundation can no man lay than that is laid, which is Jesus Christ.* (I Cor. 3:11)

Jesus Christ referred to himself as a great foundation rock when he said *"Upon this rock will I build my church,"* (Matt. 16:18).

STONES FOR A FOUNDATION

The great foundation number.

The question that God asked Job regarding the foundations of the earth provides a clue, and points the way for an exciting journey into a search for the beginning of things—The Great Foundation. During the many hours involved in this study, I was overwhelmed by the beauty of the great Master Architect who planned with precision the vast, yet minute, interwoven wonders of the creation of his universe and his far-reaching plan for his human family. At best, we are permitted to see only pieces. The finite mind cannot grasp that which is infinite. But we have been given clues that point the way—clues given to us in the Word living, the Word written, the Word in stone, the Word in number, and the Word in the cosmos. Share with me some of those little pieces!

The question God asked Job was profound.

> *Upon what are her foundation-pillars made to sink? Or who laid the cornerstone?*

About two thousand years after he posed that question, God gave a vision to the Apostle John. In describing that vision, John wrote:

> *And after these things I saw four angels standing on the four corners of the earth.* (Rev. 7:1)

The word corner, as used in the original Greek, is γωνια and has the number equivalent of 864. Four of these would be 3456. The progression of $3 \times 4 \times 5 \times 6$ equals 360, the number of degrees in a circle. Thus is combined the concept of four corners with that which is circular—the union of the circle and the square.

A circle and a square are fundamental opposites. The squaring of the circle is a mathematical impossibility.[1] However, the union of the two can be shown by a circle and square of the same perimeter. Man, as represented by the square, became estranged from God through the disobedience of Adam. The circle, however, represents perfection, and it has no beginning nor ending—a fitting symbol of God. The death of Jesus Christ as man's redeemer

---

1 The squaring of the circle is the attempt to make a square of the same area as a circle.

provided the means for the reconciliation between God and his human family—bringing into one harmonious unit the circle and the square.

Thus the vision was given to John of four angels standing on the four corners of a circular earth. Hidden in the vision was the relationship of *corner, γωνια,* 864, to a circle: 4 x 864 = 3456.

3456   The city of my God (Rev. 3:12) *της πολεως του Θεου μου*

3 x 4 x 5 x 6 = 360
360   The number of degrees in a circle.
360   The Rock that begat us (Deut. 32:18) צוּר יְלָדְךָ

Also hidden in the vision was the effect of this union. Peace! The *four corners of the earth, τεσσαρας γωνιας της γης,* has a number value of 2790. The name Salem, meaning peace, is from the Greek, *Σαλημ,* and bears the number 279.

Salem is the city of Jerusalem, *Ιερουσαλημ,* whose number equivalent is 864. The name in Hebrew means the Foundation of Peace, (Foundation, ירו , 216; Peace, שָׁלֵם, 370, making a total of 586).

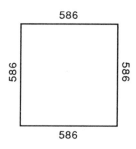

586

586   586

586

Perimeter 2344

"The majesty of God" = 2344

Change the above square to a circle of the same circumference, and draw a square tangent to that circle, and the new square has sides of 460.

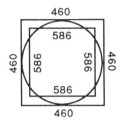

Thus the union of the circle and the square describe the place of union between God and man, Mount Moriah, מוֹרֶה הַר , 460. It was on Mount Moriah, in the city of Jerusalem (864) that the temple was built. The Rock, The Foundation upon which it was constructed, represents the great Cornerstone, γωνια, 864. The inner chamber within that temple was the Holy of Holies, αγιων, 864.

Jesus said *"The stone which the builders rejected, the same is become the head of the corner; this is the Lord's doing, it is marvellous in our eyes."* Its marvellous nature comes to light when we realize that this cornerstone, 864, or *"head of the corner"* (corner, 864) is the sum of four sides of 216—*"The stone which the builders rejected,"* λιθον ον απεδοκιμασαν οι οικοδομουντες, 2160. It was none other than the "Lion of the tribe of Judah," (Lion, אַרְיֵה , 216).

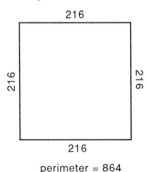

perimeter = 864

The stone which the builders rejected = 2160
is become the head of the corner = 864

By his death on Calvary he provided the means for the reconciliation between God and man—the union of the circle and the square—and the result is life, ζωην, 864.

The number 864 is a beautiful symbol of life, for it is the solar number—the diameter of the sun being 864,000 miles. The sun is the physical source of light, and life. It represents the Creator and the work of creation.[1] It is indeed the great foundation number! The name God, Θεων, has the number equivalent of 864.

The foundation number, 864, is a multiple of another foundation number, 12 (72 x 12 = 864). Twelves are used throughout holy scripture to denote foundations.

The foundation-pillars of the Great Pyramid were sunk into the bedrock at its four base corners. The rock level distance between each of these corners was 72 reeds.[2]

The number 72 also becomes a foundation number by its use in the gematria of both the Old and New Testaments. To the Greeks, rock, τοπος, bore the number 720. But the concept of a foundation becomes apparent by the use of this number with reference to the Lord Jesus Christ. He was the *seed* through whom the promise given to Jacob, (as he lay sleeping on the Bethel stone), would eventually *"bless all the families of the earth."* Seed, σπορος, has a number value of 720. He was the Great High Priest through whom the reconciliation between God and man would be accomplished. High Priest, ιερευς, bears the number 72. He declared *"I am the way, the truth, and the life." The truth, η αληθεια,* 72, when multiplied by the foundation number 12, produces 864, the great foundation number.

In the earth-moon model on page 18 the Pythagorean triangle (3:4:5) is obtained by the dimensions of earth and moon. This unique right triangle bears the number 72 both by

---

1 The concept of the sun as representing the Creator has already been shown on pages 11-14.

2 The unit of measure called the reed was given to the prophet Ezekiel by God. It measures 10.56 feet, or precisely the length of each of the stone lintels that topped the Sarsen Circle at Stonehenge. Ezekiel 40:5.

addition and by multiplication. Thus $3 + 4 + 5 = 12$, a foundation number, and $3 \times 4 \times 5 = 60$, the number that pertains to earth and man. Raise the dimension by adding $12 + 60 = 72$, or by multiplying $12 \times 60 = 720$, and the result is the number of Truth, 72. The dimension can be raised one more time thus:

$$3{:}4{:}5 \left\{ \begin{array}{l} 720 \times 3 = 2160 \\ 720 \times 4 = 2880 \\ 720 \times 5 = 3600 \end{array} \right. \qquad \begin{array}{r} 2160 \\ +\ 2880 \\ +\ \underline{3600} \\ 8640 \end{array}$$

The 3:4:5 triangle, known today as the Pythagorean triangle, is considered the single most important theorem in the whole of mathematics, because it establishes a fundamental characterization of both time and space, and the laws that bind the universe. Pythagoras had discovered a divine truth. It does not appear to be coincidence that the name of this ancient Greek philosopher and mathematician would have the number equivalent of 864, Πυθαγορας.

864,000 miles - diameter of the sun
864   Jerusalem, Ιερουσαλημ
864   Cornerstone, γωνια
864   Holy of Holies, αγιων
864   life, ζωην
864   corner, γωνια
864   saints, αγιων
864   flock of God, ποιμνιον Θεου
864   Pythagoras, Πυθαγορας
864   God, Θεων

Twelve foundations.

The figure 12 is used throughout the Bible to denote the concept of foundations.

The 12 sons of Jacob became the foundation-pillars of Israel. The 12 apostles became the foundation-pillars of Christianity. Both of these foundation illustrations were used to describe the

Holy City that the Apostle John saw in vision.

> *He carried me away in the spirit to a great and high mountain, and showed me that great city, the holy Jerusalem, descending out of heaven from God, having the glory of God.* (Revelation 21:10)

What a magnificent sight! The beauty of the city was so overwhelming to John that his response was to fall on his face and worship the holy messenger who talked with him. But the messenger rebuked him, and assured him that the reverence, the worship, and the thanksgiving were due to God alone.

John's description of the city that he saw has captured the imagination of everyone who has ever studied his Revelation. The name of the city was Jerusalem, 864, but not the old Jerusalem where God's typical kingdom had been established. This was the new Jerusalem, where his long-promised glorious kingdom would engulf the whole world. The graphic word picture that he paints is obviously not sufficient to describe fully the glory and beauty of what he saw, for how can divine things be described by human words? Yet the words are still effective in describing that which is more beautiful and more glorious than any human has ever imagined. He describes it thus:

> *... and her light was like unto a stone most precious, even like a jasper stone, clear as crystal; and had a wall great and high, and had twelve gates, and at the gates twelve angels, and names written thereon, which are the names of the twelve tribes of the children of Israel: on the east three gates; on the north three gates; on the south three gates; and on the west three gates.*
>
> *And the wall of the city had twelve foundations, and in them the names of the twelve apostles of the Lamb. And he that talked with me had a golden reed to measure the city, and the gates thereof, and the wall thereof.*
>
> *And the city lieth four-square, and the length is as large as the breadth: and he measured the city with the reed,*

twelve thousand furlongs. The length and the breadeth and the height of it are equal. And he measured the wall thereof, an hundred and forty and four cubits, according to the measure of a man, that is, of the angel.

And the building of the wall of it was of jasper: and the city was pure gold, like unto clear glass.

And the foundations of the wall of the city were garnished with all manner of precious stones. The first foundation was jasper; the second, sapphire; the third, a chalcedony; the fourth, an emerald; the fifth, sardonyx; the sixth, sardius; the seventh, chrysolyte; the eighth, beryl; the ninth, a topaz; the tenth, a chrysoprasus; the eleventh, a jacinth; the twelfth, an amethyst.

And the twelve gates were twelve pearls; every several gate was of one pearl; and the street of the city was pure gold, as it were transparent glass.

And I saw no temple therein: for the Lord God Almighty and the Lamb are the temple of it. And the city had no need of the sun, neither of the moon, to shine in it: for the glory of God did lighten it, and the Lamb is the light thereof.

And the nations shall walk in the light of it: and the kings of the earth do bring their glory into it. And they shall bring the glory of the nations into it.

And there shall in no wise enter into it anything that defileth, neither whatsoever worketh abomination, or maketh a lie: but they which are written in the Lamb's book of life.

This beautiful city is characterized by six sets of 12, or 6 x 12 = 72. It had 12 gates, bearing 12 pearls, on which were written the names of the 12 tribes, guarded by 12 angels; and 12 foundations bearing the names of the 12 apostles. Thus it bears all three foundation numbers, 12; 6 x 12 = 72; 72 x 12 = 864.

Its dimensions are also characterized by 12; for each side of its square base measured 12,000 furlongs, and its wall was 144 cubits (12 x 12 = 144).

The city was a cube, thus 12,000 furlongs linear measure per side would be 144,000 square furlongs on each face, giving a total surface area of 864,000 square furlongs, (6 x 144,000 = 864,000).

The wall is not only given in a different unit of measure (cubits), but it is also to a different scale. Using the royal cubit, as shown in the Great Pyramid to be 1.72 feet, this circular wall would be about 248 feet. Since suggesting this in my previous book,[1] it has been called to my attention that the length of the unit of measure was codified in the gematria that was given to John.

And there was given me a reed like a rod. (Rev. 11:1)

The actual numerical value for the *"reed like a rod,"* καλαμος ομολος ραβδω, is 1729, however, the rules of gematria (see Appendix I) would suggest that this is equivalent to 1728, which is 12^3. If this symbolic *"reed like a rod"* were used to measure the circular wall of the New Jerusalem, the circumference would be 248832 feet, without placing a decimal point.

The irrational nature of the π ratio (3.14159+) has, in ancient times, been stated as a rational fraction. The more accurate of the several fractions used was 864/275. Because of the beautiful symbolic nature of the number 864, I tried this formula for π with the above circumference of the New Jerusalem wall, and the result is a diameter of 79200 feet.

The city is described as a cube of 12,000 furlongs per side. When the scale of the circular wall is brought commensurate with the city, and stated in the same unit—feet—a remarkable picture develops. The wall is identical to the earth-circumference, and the city is commensurate with the square drawn on the earth-circumference, as was shown in the earth-moon model on page 18. This creates the suggestion that the wall was not only circular, it was spherical.

This wall, with its 12 beautiful precious stones for foundations, seems to engulf the earth. The conditions described within that city would seem to describe conditions that would engulf the earth. John described it thus:

---

1 *Stonehenge ...a closer look,* Bonnie Gaunt, page 129.

And I, John, saw the holy city, the New Jerusalem, coming down from God out of heaven, prepared as a bride adorned for her husband.

And I heard a great voice out of heaven saying, ""Behold, the tabernacle of God is with men, and he will dwell with them, and they shall be his people, and God himself shall be their God. And God shall wipe away all tears from their eyes; and there shall be no more death, neither sorrow nor crying, neither shall there be any more pain: for the former things are passed away."

And he that sat upon the throne said, "Behold, I make all things new."

John seems to have seen the same thing that the prophet Isaiah had described some 700 years previously:

And the ransomed of the Lord shall return, and come to Zion, with songs and everlasting joy upon their heads: they shall obtain joy and gladness, and sorrow and sighing shall flee away. (Isaiah 35:10)

And the work of righteousness shall be peace: and the effect of righteousness quietness and assurance forever. And my people shall dwell in a peaceable habitation, and in sure dwellings, and in quiet resting places. (Isaiah 32:17, 18)

It is a beautiful word picture of the kingdom for which Jesus taught his disciples to pray:

Thy kingdom come, thy will be done on earth as it is in heaven.

The voice that spoke to John said, *"The tabernacle of God is with men."* It is describing the condition of full reconciliation between God and man, as is illustrated by the circle and the square. *"He will dwell with them, and they shall be his people, and God himself shall be with them, and be their God."* It will be the fulfilling of the covenant that had been confirmed to Jacob as he rested his head on the Bethel Rock—*"In thy seed shall all the families of the earth be blessed."* The following demonstration of gematria shows the beauty and harmony of the promise.

1584   I will establish my covenant, וַהֲקִמֹתִי אֶת־בְּרִיתִי

1584   In Isaac shall thy seed be called (Rom. 9:7), *εν Ισαακ κληθησεται σοι σπερμα*

The number 1584 is 132 multiplied by the foundation number, 12 (12 x 32 = 1584). The number 132 tells the same story. It tells of a stone cut out of the mountains that grew and became a glorious kingdom that filled the whole earth. It tells of the time when the kingdoms would belong to Jehovah, and he would make mankind whole again.

132   make whole, *ιαομια*

1320   The stone cut out of the mountains (Daniel 2:45)
       מִטּוּרָא אִתְגְּזֶרֶת אֶבֶן

132   The kingdom is Jehovah's (Psalm 22:28)
       יְהוָה הַמְּלוּכָה

132   Jehovah your God (Joshua 4:5) יְהוָה אֱלֹהֵיכֶם

The prophecy goes on to say that this stone became a great mountain and filled the whole earth. This *"stone"* kingdom will *"never be destroyed"* because *"it shall stand forever,"* (Daniel 2:35 & 44).

The prophet Isaiah described some of the conditions of that mountain.

> *And he (God) will destroy in this mountain the covering cast over all people (death).... He will swallow up death in victory, and the Lord God will wipe away tears from off all faces...and it shall be said in that day, This is our God...we have waited for him, we will be glad and rejoice*

in his salvation, for in this mountain shall the hand of the Lord rest.

The prophet Micah also spoke of this mountain, and connected it with the holy Jerusalem.

Come, let us go up to the mountain of the Lord, to the house of the God of Jacob, and he will teach us of his ways, and we will walk in his paths: for the law shall go forth of Zion, and the word of the Lord from Jerusalem. (Micah 4:2)

It was thrilling to find that the gematria for *"the word of the Lord from Jerusalem,"* וּדְבַר יְהֹוָה מִירוּשָׁלָ‍ִם , is 864. Is there any doubt that Micah was describing the New Jerusalem as it encompasses the whole earth!

By the rules of gematria, the New Jerusalem, καινης Ιερουσαλημ, (Rev. 3:12) bears the number 1152. This was pictured by the stone cut out of the mountain that grew and filled the whole earth. The concept of *"hewn out of the rock,"* μησεν εν πετρα, has a number equivalent of 1152. The number for *"Kingdom of God,"* η βασιλειαν Θεου, is 1152 (Matthew 21:31), or την βασιλειαν Θεου, also 1152. The *"Kingdom of heaven,"* βασιλεια των ουραναν, in Matthew 13:47 bears the number 2880; how beautiful to realize that a square with sides of 288 has a perimeter of 1152:

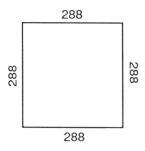

Perimeter 1152

103

THE STONES CRY OUT

Many of the prophets of old wrote of the beauty of that glorious Kingdom which would engulf the whole earth. It was said of Abraham that *"he looked for a city which hath foundations, whose builder and maker is God,"* (Hebrews 11:10). The *"city which hath foundations"* is the New Jerusalem, whose wall encompasses the earth, and whose foundations are 12 precious stones.

The earth commensurate New Jerusalem can be shown graphically by the diagram below.

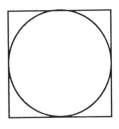

The New Jerusalem
Perimeter 48,000 furlongs, or31,680,000 feet
Diameter of wall 7,920,000 feet
Circumference of wall 24,881,392 feet

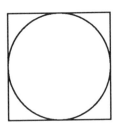

The Earth
Perimeter of square 31,680 miles
Diameter of earth 7,920 miles
Circumference of earth 24,881,392 miles

The relationship of the New Jerusalem to the earth is remarkable, for it is exact, but in a different unit—the former in feet, the latter in miles.

Even more remarkable is the fact that the builder of Stonehenge, 4,000 years ago, erected stones in a circular configuration whose dimensions are precisely commensurate with the earth and the New Jerusalem.

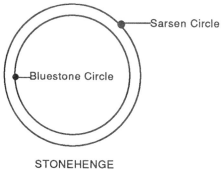

STONEHENGE

Circumference of Sarsen Circle 316.8 feet
Diameter of Bluestone Circle 79.2 feet
Circumference of Bluestone Circle 248.81392 feet

If we were to bring the New Jerusalem and Stonehenge to the same scale, one would overlay the other as in the diagram below.

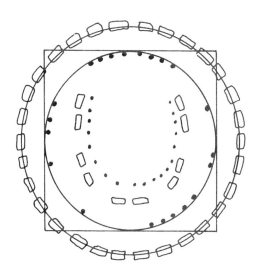

Did man 4,000 years ago know the dimensions of the earth; or did he know the dimensions of the New Jerusalem? The vision and the dimensions were not given to John until A.D. 90! Or was the design of Stonehenge of divine origin, placed there as a witness of the promise of the New Jerusalem—the Kingdom of God that would engulf the whole earth!

Stonehenge, the Great Pyramid, and the union of the Circle and the Square.

Four thousand years ago, on that lonely, windswept plain in the southern part of a remote island we now call England, the demonstration of the union of the circle and the square was permanently written in stone by the relationship of the Sarsen Circle to the Bluestone Circle at Stonehenge. It is the bringing together of two fundamental opposites into one harmonious whole. It pre-figured the great reconciliation between God and man that will encompass the whole earth— the New Jerusalem.

The union of the circle and square at Stonehenge can be shown graphically thus:

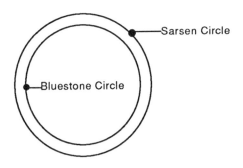

Change the Sarsen Circle to a square of the same perimeter, and it would be tangent to the Bluestone Circle as shown in the following diagram:

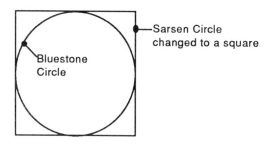

It is the fundamental principle as shown in the earth-moon model on page 18. It has been demonstrated that the geometry of these two circles at Stonehenge is identical to the geometry of the earth, and the New Jerusalem, using the same numbers, but to different scales.

This principle of the union of the circle and the square can be found over and over again in the geometry and gematria of Stonehenge, the Great Pyramid, the Earth, and the Holy Scriptures. Below are two examples that I found to be thrilling in the story they tell. They confirm the concept of the reconciliation of God and man in that earth-encompassing kingdom of peace called the New Jerusalem. In each, the progression is formed by starting with a square, superimposing a circle whose circumference is the same as the square, (just as was done with Stonehenge and the New Jerusalem), then drawing a new square tangent to that circle. Then repeating the function.

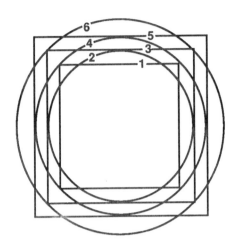

1. One Side 864

   .00864 Megalithic Miles, circumference of inmost
   configuration of stones at Stonehenge[1].

   864   The great foundation number

   864   Jerusalem, $Ιερουσαλημ$

   864   He shall reign (Rev. 11:15), $βασιλευσει$

   864   The word of the Lord from Jerusalem (Micah 4:2),
   וּדְבַר יְהוָה מִירוּשָׁלַ͏ִם

   864   Cornerstone, $γωνια$

   864   Holy of Holies, $αγιων$

   864   Life, $ζωην$

   864   Saints, $αγιων$

   864   Flock of God, $ποιμνιον\ Θεου$

   864   Corner, $γωνια$

   864   God, $Θεων$

---

1 The megalithic mile is a unit found by A. Thom in his studies at Stonehenge
and other megalithic sites in Britain; it is equal to 2.727272 miles or 14,400 feet.
Thus the diameter of the sun, 864,000 miles, could be stated as 316,800 megalithic miles, bearing the number of Lord Jesus Christ. The rock level base of the
Great Pyramid shows the relationship of the megalithic mile to the British mile,
for one of its sides measures .05280 megalithic mile.

2. Circumference 3456

   3456   square megalithic miles, surface area of sphirical wall of the New Jerusalem

   3456   City of my God (Rev. 3:12), $\tau\eta\varsigma\ \pi o\lambda\varepsilon\omega\varsigma\ \tau o\upsilon\ \Theta\varepsilon o\upsilon\ \mu o\upsilon$

   3456   The marriage of the Bride and Lamb (Rev. 19:7), $\alpha\ \gamma\alpha\mu o\varsigma\ \tau o\upsilon\ \alpha\rho\nu\iota o\upsilon\ \kappa\alpha\iota\ \eta\ \gamma\upsilon\nu\eta\ \alpha\upsilon\tau o\upsilon$

   3456   Ye are the temple of God, $\alpha\ \varpi\alpha o\varsigma\ \tau o\upsilon\ \Theta\varepsilon o\upsilon\ \alpha\iota\tau\iota\nu\varepsilon\varsigma\ \varepsilon\sigma\tau\varepsilon\ \upsilon\mu\varepsilon\iota\sigma$

   3 x 4 x 5 x 6 = 360, the number of degrees in a circle

   360   the rock that begat us (Deut. 32:18) צוּר יְלָדְךָ

   3600 The Lamb's book of life, $\tau\omega\ \beta\iota\beta\lambda\iota\omega\ \zeta\omega\eta\varsigma\ \alpha\pi\nu\iota o\upsilon$

2. Diameter 1100
3. One side 1100

   110   foundation מוּסָד

   110   stone (Rev. 9:20), $\lambda\iota\theta\iota\nu\alpha$

   1100 unexcelling greatness (Eph. 1:19), $\upsilon\pi\varepsilon\rho\beta\alpha\lambda\lambda o\nu\ \mu\varepsilon\gamma\varepsilon\theta o\varsigma$

   11   world, $\gamma\eta$

   11   earth, $\gamma\eta$

   11   gold דְּהַב

   110   your King, (Zech. 9:9) מַלְכֵּךְ

3. Perimeter 4400
4. Circumference 4400

   44   blood (the means of man's redemption),

   44   lamb (the Lamb of God who shed his blood for man), בֶּן

   440 perfect (the condition of the one who shed his blood), תֹּם

   440 mountain (symbol of the New Jerusalem), $o\rho o\varsigma$

   44   Jehovah lives (Psalm 18:45), חַי־יְהוָה

4. Diameter 1400

5. One side 1400

    140   redemption פְּדְיוֹם

    1400 Holy City (Rev. 22:19), πολεως αγιας

    14   gold זָהָב

    140   Prince נָסִיךְ

    1400 worship, θεραπευω

5. Perimeter 5600

6. Circumference 5600

    56   Golden City מַרְהֵבָה

    56   forever יוֹם

    56   whole יוֹם

    560 saints of the Most High (Dan. 7:18), קַדִּישֵׁי עֶלְיוֹנִין

    560 blessed be Jehovah my Rock (Psalm 144:1),
        בָּרוּךְ יְהוָה צוּרִי

On the opposite page is a further demonstration of the same geometric principle, using as the foundation, the base measure of the Great Pyramid.

110

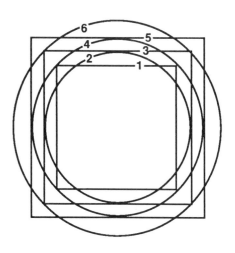

1. One side 365.242

   365.242   number of days in solar tropical year.

   365.242 sacred cubits—one side of base of Great Pyramid
   at socket level.

1. Perimeter 1460
2. Circumference 1460

   146 sacred cubits—height of topstone of Great Pyramid

   146   everlasting, עוֹלָם

   146   a precious cornerstone, a sure foundation,
   פִּנַּת יִקְרַת מוּסָד מוּסָד

   146   Jehovah-nisse, יְהוָֹה נִסִּי

   146   world (without end), עוֹלָם

2. Diameter 465
3. One side 465

   465   every nation (Rev. 14:6), παν εθνος

   465   City of Refuge (picture of complete redemption through
   Christ), עיר מקלטו

3. Perimeter 1860
4. Circumference 1860
   186,000   speed of light
   186   Jehovah is my Rock (Psa. 18:2), יְהוָה סַלְעִי
   186   His work (Deut. 32:4), פָּעֳלוֹ
   186   Great Rock (Isa. 32:1), סֶלַע־כָּבֵד
   186   Golgotha (place of union between God and man)
         Γολγοθα

4. Diameter 592
5. One side 592
   592   The stone shall become the house of God (the Bethel
         Stone), והאבן יהיה בית אלהים
   592   holiness, αγλοτης
   592   Godhead, Θεοτης

5. Perimeter 2368
6. Circumference 2368
   2368   Jesus Christ, Ιησους Χριστος
   2368   The God of Gods, ο Θεος των Θεων
   2368   Holy of Holies, ο αγιος των αγιων

The above demonstration of the union of the circle and the
square could in no way be contrived by man. Its accuracy is far
beyond the possibility of coincidence. I believe it is a brief
glimpse into the vast and intricate workings of the Master
Mathematician—the Creator!

6

The Stones of a Crown

"The Lord their God shall save them in that day as the flock of his people: for they shall be as the stones of a crown, lifted up as an ensign upon his land." (Zech. 9:16)

The concept of a crown, and the stones of a crown, is used frequently in the scriptures—both Old and New Testaments—and the time frame is always in relation to the reconciliation of God and man.

The prophet Isaiah worded it beautifully when he said:

> *Thou shalt be called by a new name, which the mouth of the Lord shall name. Thou shalt also be a crown of glory in the hand of the Lord, and a royal diadem in the hand of thy God.* (Isaiah 62:3, 4)

The *crown of glory,* עֲטֶרֶת תִּפְאֶרֶת has a number equivalent of 1760, and *a royal diadem,* מְלוּכָה וּצְנִיף has the number 333. The gematria seems not to be coincidence, for these two numbers have a remarkable relationship to the reconciliation between God and man.

The prophet Ezekiel, while captive in Babylon, was given a vision of a beautiful temple. Although that temple was never actually constructed, the specifications were given to him in detail. In the vision he saw his God dwelling in that beautiful temple; he saw a river of life-giving water flowing from beneath the temple; and he saw a beautiful city. In the vision he was transported to a high hill, as it were, where he could look down on this magnificent sight.

113

To Ezekiel, separated from his homeland and his people, it was the confirmation of all that he had lived for—the assurance that God was in the Temple and there was indeed a meeting place between God and Man. To students of the Old Testament, the vision is a promise of redemption from the Adamic death-curse, and a reconciliation to God. It is a beautiful picture of the relationship of man to his Creator during and beyond earth's great millennium.

The length, as well as the breadth, of that beautiful Temple was 176 feet.[1] The *crown of glory* bears the number 1760.

While still in vision, Ezekiel looked down from his vantage point and saw a city to the south, in the portion of land that was set aside as an offering to God. The holy portion of land was a square, measuring 25,000 great cubits per side, giving a perimeter of 33.3 miles. The *royal diadem* bears the number 333.

This holy portion of land that was an offering to God, also bore His number—*God the Saviour, Θεω τω σωτηρι,* 3330.

The city Ezekiel saw to the south is commensurate in its measurements with the New Jerusalem, Stonehenge, and the geometry of the earth. Its perimeter was 18,000 great cubits, or 31,680 feet. It pictures the reconciliation of God and man, and it bears the number of the one who made that reconciliation possible—the Lord Jesus Christ, *Κυριος Ιησους Χριστος,* 3168.

---

1 The Great Cubit given to Ezekiel by God was a unit measuring 1.76 British Feet. The Reed, by which Ezekiel was told to measure the temple, was six Great Cubits, or a length of 10.56 feet. This standard was used at Stonehenge: the mean length of each of the carefully tooled lintels that topped the Sarsen Circle was 10.56 feet. There is evidence that this unit was known to the builders of Stonehenge, for most of its geometry is evenly divisible by 1.76. The origin of the Great Cubit is discussed more fully in *Stonehenge...a closer look* by Bonnie Gaunt, pages 215 - 219.

7

The Stones Cry Out
Epilogue

Surely stones have been the mouthpiece through which God has spoken to man—the instrument through which he has concealed and revealed his plan of the ages. A plan that touches the lives of every one of us. No wonder Jesus used those remarkable words *"If these should hold their peace, the stones would immediately cry out."*

They were not idle words, for the gematria of that phrase has a striking relationship to God's plan of the ages.

$$The\ stones\ cry\ out,\ οι\ λιθοι\ κραξουσιν = 1120$$
$$9\ \text{x}\ 1120 = 10080$$
$$5\ \text{x}\ 1120 = 5600$$

The earth-moon model shown on page 18 is repeated below to show the certainty with which Jesus chose those words. The height of the entire model is 10080 miles. The figure is all-encompassing, as was shown by the words of the Psalmist, *"The work of Thy fingers,"* מַעֲשֵׂי אֶצְבְּעֹתֶיךָ, 1008. David was speaking of the work of the whole creation of God. How beautiful to find in Revelation 15:3 the ones who are praising God for this wonderful creation also bear the number 10080:

10080 *"And they sing the song of Moses, the servant of God, and the song of the Lamb,"* και αδουσιν την ωδην Μωυσεωσ του δουλου του Θεου και την ωδην του αρνιου

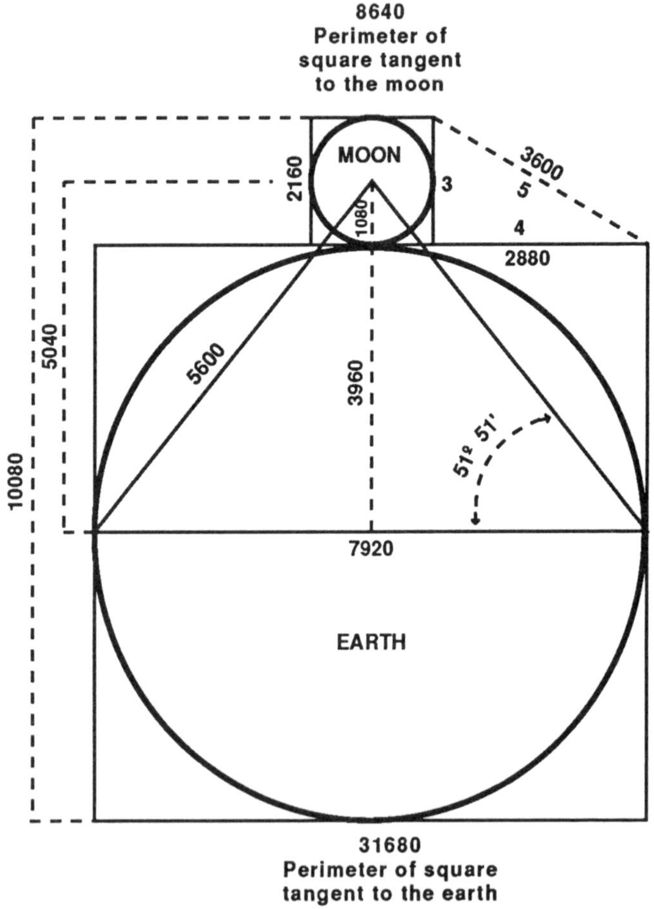

8640
Perimeter of
square tangent
to the moon

MOON

2160

1080

3

3600

5

4

2880

5600

3960

10080

5040

51° 51'

7920

EARTH

31680
Perimeter of square
tangent to the earth

Distances are in miles.

The pyramid that is constructed on the radii of earth and moon has a height of 5040 miles and a side angled verticle of 5600 miles. That pyramid bears the precise proportions of the Great Pyramid in Egypt—a pyramid whose stones indeed cry out to be heard, for it is a witness of all the works of God.

"The stones cry out," when written in Hebrew (Habakkuk 2:11) אֶבֶן מִקִּיר has a number equivalent of 630. When this figure is multiplied by the figure that represents the life-giving work of Jesus, 8, the product is 5040, (8 x 630 = 5040), as is shown in the height of this earth commensurate pyramid. When the same words are written in Greek, οι λιθοι κραξουσιν, the number equivalent is 1120. This figure, multiplied by 5 gives the product of 5600, as shown in the side angled vertical.[1]

The words of the one who rode the young colt up the steep hill to Jerusalem that warm spring day over 2,000 years ago, still ring throughout the ages—the stones cry out!

---

1 The number 5 pertains to Jesus as earth's rightful ruler. In Hebrew the word ruler is 500; prince, 500; to restore, 500.

The Great Pyramid

APPENDIX I

Gematria

"To whom then will ye liken God? or what likeness will ye compare to him?...Have ye not known? have ye not heard? hath it not been told you from the beginning? have ye not understanding from the foundation of the earth? It is He that sitteth upon the circle of the earth...; that stretcheth out the heavens as a curtain, and spreadeth them out as a tent to dwell in.... Lift up your eyes on high, and behold who hath created these things, that bringeth out their host by number..." (Isaiah 40:18-26)

All creation, from the largest to the smallest, can always be reduced to numbers. Pythagoras, the father of mathematics, discovered a great truth when he observed, "numbers are the language of the universe." In the writings of the ancient philosophers there is common agreement that the purpose of number is for the investigation of the universe. From the atom to the galaxy in the heavens, the same unchanging laws apply—the laws of arithmetic, the language of number.

Just as the hand of God spread the vast expanse of the heavens by number, so too his written word can be reduced to number; and those who have tried it have stood in awe of the intricacy and beauty of the design. It was an intentional design.

In the year 547 B.C., Daniel, a Hebrew captive in Babylon, saw a vision which carried him into the vast unknown future. At the conclusion of the vision he saw what appeared to be an angel speak to another angel and ask concerning the time when the vision would be fulfilled. The second heavenly personage was called, in Hebrew, Palmoni, פלמוני, The Wonderful Numberer, or The Numberer of Secrets. His very name has a number equivalent of 216—a number which we have seen (page 19) relates to *Kingdom of the Father, βασιλεια των πατρος,* 2160 (Matt. 13.43).

The secrets locked up in numbers in the Old and New Testaments are there for all to behold; and down through the centuries many have unlocked those secrets and revealed to us the unspeakable beauty of the intended design. Part of the numerical design of the scriptures is the science of gematria.

The Old Testament was originally written in the Hebrew language, and the New Testament in Greek. These two languages were unique among languages in that every letter of their alphabets had a double meaning—a meaning of sound, and a meaning of number. It was a "dual character system."

Tobias Dantzig, a professor of mathematics at the University of Maryland (U.S.A.) explained the phenomenon thus.[1]

> The sum of the numbers represented by the letters of the word was the number of the word, and from the standpoint of Gematria two words were equivalent if they added up to the same number. Not only was Gematria used from the earliest days for the interpretation of Biblical passages, but there are indications that the writers of the Bible had practiced the art. Thus Abraham proceeding to rescue his brother Eliasar drives forth 318 slaves. Is it just a coincidence that the Hebrew word Eliasar adds up to 318?

In the Cyclopaedia of Biblical, Theological and Ecclesiastical Literature, by John McClintoch and James Strong (1880) similar expression is given to the use of gematria. In Volume IX, page 479, in their explanation of various methods for the interpretation of scripture, the following is stated:

> … the Scripture was explained according to the *Notaricon,* or according to *Gematria,* a word borrowed from the Greek, either corresponding to γεωμετρια or γραμματεια. The idea of this rule was, since every letter is a numeral, to reduce the word to the number it contains, and to explain the word by another of the same quantity. Thus from the words "Lo! three men stood by him" (Gen. xvii, 2), it is deduced that these three angels were *Michael, Gabriel,*

---

1 Tobias Dantzig, *Number, the Language of Science,* Doubleday Anchor Books, New York, NY, 1930, p. 40.

and *Raphael,* because והנה שלשה, *and lo! three men,* and אלו מיכאל גבריאל ורפאל, *these are Michael, Gabriel, and Raphael,* are of the same numerical value, as will be seen from the following reduction to their numerical value of both these phrases:

ה ש ל ש ה נ ה י
5+300+30+300+5+50+5+6=701.

ל א י ר ב ג ל א כ י מ ו ל א
30+1+10+200+2+3+30+1+20+10+40+6+30+1

ל פ א ר ו
+30+1+80+200+6=701.

Thus McClintock and Strong verify the authenticity of the use of gematria in scripture, showing that it is indeed a method for interpretation.

One of the best known demonstrations of gematria in the Old Testament is the section headings in Psalm 119. Any student of the Old Testament is aware that the names for these sections are in fact the sequential letters of the Hebrew alphabet. These letters were simply used to number the sections. In some Bibles the word for the letter is spelled out, (such as *aleph*); while in other translations, the single letter is used (such as א)—both of these translate, by gematria, to the number 1.

A lesser known example of gematria is the number 666 in Revelation 13:18. The original Greek manuscripts simply wrote this as three letters of the alphabet, which, given their number equivalents, added up to 666.

Gematria among the Greeks was in common use at the time of the writing of the New Testament. A copy of one of these early manuscripts, called *papyri,* (because they were written on papyrus) exists today in Dublin, Ireland in the Chester Beatty Collection. It is the earliest known copy of the book of Revelation extant. It is dated somewhere between 200 and 300 A.D. This manuscript uses gematria for every number in the book of Revelation, rather than Arabic numerals as we have in our modern translations. For example, every time the number 7 appears, it is written as ζ, which is the letter *zeta,* having a number value of 7.

APPENDIX I

In this *papyri,* not only the number 666 is written in gematria, but the beloved number 144. Describing the number of those who stood with the Lamb on Mount Zion, it gives it as $\rho\mu\delta$ (ρ=100; μ=40; δ=4), followed by the Greek word for thousands.

The discovery of these number codes is not new. The noted Bible expositor, E. W. Bullinger, was among the many who have added to our understanding of this subject. His book *Number in Scripture,* published in 1894, shows the supernatural design in the use of numbers, both in the works of God and in the word of God. Another expositor, Ivan Panin, published his "Bible Numerics" articles in 1912. More recently published is the exciting work of Jerry Lucas and Del Washburn, *Theomatics,* (Stein & Day, New York, 1977). The name means "God's Numbers." In fact, the number equivalents for the Greek alphabet can be found in any Webster's Dictionary.

The Greek alphabet uses twenty six letters, two of which have become extinct. Their number values appear below:

Alpha	α	1
Beta	β	2
Gamma	γ	3
Delta	δ	4
Epsilon	ε	5
Zeta	ζ	7
Eta	η	8
Theta	θ	9
Iota	ι	10
Kappa	κ	20
Lambda	λ	30
Mu	μ	40
Nu	ν	50
Xi	ξ	60
Omicron	o	70
Pi	π	80
Rho	ρ	100
Sigma	σ . ς	200
Tau	τ	300
Upsilon	υ	400
Phi	φ	500
Chi	χ	600
Psi	ψ	700
Omega	ω	800

There were once letters for 6 and 90, but they became obsolete through time. The letter standing for the number 6 fell entirely out of use, and was occasionally substituted by the symbol ς', which looks much like *sigma, ς*, but differs by the addition of the accent. The only use of the symbol for 6 in the entire New Testament is in Revelation 13:18, the number of the Beast, $X\xi\varsigma = 600, 60, 6$. If the letter that appears as *sigma* were given the value of *sigma*, 200, the number of the Beast would be 860. It is interesting that the Beast, who is an imposter, attempts to bear the number for God, *elohim,* אלהים 86.

The best known name in the New Testament is Lord Jesus Christ. The gematria for his name is demonstrated thus:

K = 20	ι = 10	X = 600
υ = 400	η = 8	ρ = 100
ρ = 100	σ = 200	ι = 10
ι = 10	ο = 70	σ = 200
ο = 70	υ = 400	τ = 300
s = 200	s = 200	ο = 70
800	888	s = 200
		1480

Lord (800) Jesus (888) Christ (1480) = 3168

As has been shown, this number is also given to the mean circumference of the Sarsen Circle at Stonehenge (316.8 feet), the perimeter of a square drawn tangent to the earth (31680 miles), the perimeter of the ground plan of the New Jerusalem (31,680,000 feet), the perimeter of the Cities of Refuge (316,800 inches), and to the perimeter of Ezekiel's City, (31680 feet).

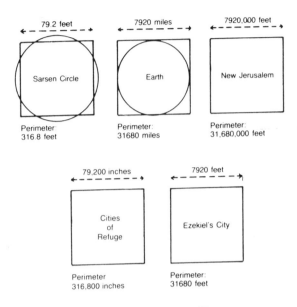

Lord Jesus Christ, $\mathrm{K}\upsilon\rho\iota o\varsigma\ \text{'}I\eta\sigma o\upsilon\varsigma\ X\rho\iota\sigma\tau o\varsigma$, 3168

When all the factors of 3168 are added together, the sum is 6660. The nature of the Beast is again shown to be an imposter.

The subject, however, is a complicated one, for the scripture reads:

> *Here is wisdom, let him that hath understanding count the number of the beast: for it is the number of a man; and his number is six hundred threescore and six.*

The final phrase *"and his number is six hundred threescore and six,"* $\kappa\alpha\iota\ o\ \alpha\rho\iota\theta\mu o\varsigma\ \alpha\upsilon\tau o\upsilon\ X\xi\varsigma$, surprisingly adds up to 2368—a figure which we have seen is the number for Jesus Christ, $I\eta\sigma o\upsilon\varsigma\ X\rho\iota\sigma\tau o\varsigma = 2368$. Through the numerical code of the scriptures, we are given the clear evidence that the Beast is an imposter, bearing the *"number of a man,"* —the man on the cross.

It has been shown that the topstone of the Great Pyramid represents Jesus, and that one of the Biblical descriptions of this topstone is *"the head of the corner."* (Matt. 21:42; Mark 12:10; Luke 20:17; I Peter 2:7) The gematria for that appellation is 666. The number first applies to the man Christ Jesus, and secondly, to his impersonator and imposter, the one who bears his number in Revelation 13:18.

The nature of the imposter is again shown by the evidence of gematria:

$$2260 = \text{Man of Sin, } o \ \alpha\nu\theta\rho\omega\pi\text{os} \ \tau\eta\text{s} \ \alpha\nu\text{o}\mu\iota\alpha\text{s}$$
$$2260 = \text{Son of Man, } o \ \upsilon\iota\text{os} \ \alpha\nu\theta\rho\omega\pi\text{ou}$$
$$2260 = \text{Image of the Beast, } \eta \ \epsilon\iota\kappa\omega\nu \ \tau\text{ou} \ \theta\eta\rho\iota\text{ou}$$

Hebrew, the language of the Old Testament, also used the alphabet as a numbering system. Their alphabet had twenty two letters, whose number equivalents are listed below:

א	'Aleph	. . . .	1
ב	Bêyth	. . . .	2
ג	Giymel	. . . .	3
ד	Dâleth	. . . .	4
ה	Hê'	. . . .	5
ו	Vâv	. . . .	6
ז	Zayin	. . . .	7
ח	Chêyth	. . . .	8
ט	Têyth	. . . .	9
י	Yôwd	. . . .	10
כ, final ך	Kaph	. . . .	20
ל	Lâmed	. . . .	30
מ, final ם	Mêm	. . . .	40
נ, final ן	Nûwn	. . . .	50
ס	Çâmek	. . . .	60
ע	'Ayin	. . . .	70
פ, final ף	Phê'	. . . .	80
פ	Pê'		·
צ, final ץ	Tsâdêy	. . . .	90
ק	Qôwph	. . . .	100
ר	Rêysh	. . . .	200
שׂ	Sîyn	. . . .	300
שׁ	Shîyn		
ת	Thâv	. . . .	400
ת	Tâv		

APPENDIX I

It should be noted that according to the rules of gematria, one or two units called *colel,* could be added or subtracted from a word without changing its meaning. In this book I have avoided the use of *colel* except in a few instances where the relationship was so powerful as to make its use obvious.

To those who study the gematria of the Bible, the use of the same number in both the Hebrew and Greek is a special joy to find, for it confirms the intended number. A prime example of this is the word *whole,* which bears the number 370 both in the Hebrew and the Greek.

370   whole,   שָׁלֵם
370   whole,   ολος

That 37 should represent wholeness is beautiful, because it is a prime number, complete in itself, divisible only by 1. But more than this, 37 is a prime factor in the titles of Jesus—the very embodiment of wholeness—a perfect man. In fact, the word *perfect* in the Old Testament,   שָׁלֵם   , has the number value of 370. Share with me the beauty of this number.

37 x 10   perfect, שָׁלֵם
37   strength, אגל
37   glory, הַכָּבוֹד
37 x 2   eternity, עַד
37 x 3   Wonderful (Isaiah 9:6), פֶּלֶא
37 x 10   peace *(shalom),* שָׁלֵם
37 x 10   ruler, מָשַׁל
37   only son, הַיָּחִיד
37 x 80   Son of Man, υιος του ανθρωπου
37 x 24   Jesus, Ιησους
37 x 84   Name of the holy child Jesus,
          ονοματος του αγιου παιδος Ιησου
37 x 40   Christ Χριστος
37 x 64   Jesus Christ, Ιησους Χριστος
37 x 120   The Lord Christ, τω κυριω Χριστω
37 x 102   My beloved Son in whom I am well pleased,
          ο υιος αγαπητος μου εις ον εγω ευδοκησα

37 x 69 Name of the only begotten Son of God,
          ονομα μονογενους υιου Θεου
37 x 66 The Son of God, τη υιου του Θεου
37 x 5   Rabbi, ο ραββι
37 x 25 The Messiah, τον Μεσσιαν
37 x 6   Nazarene, Ναζαρηνε
37 x 8   Only begotten, μονογενη
37 x 15 Our Lord and His Christ,
          κυριου ημων και του Χριστου αυτου
37 x 16 holiness, αγιοτης
37 x 18 the head of the corner ,(Psalm 118:22) לְרֹאשׁ פִּנָּה
37 x 21 the man child, (Rev. 12:13) τον αρσενα
37 x 24 I am the life, ειμι η ζωη
37 x 33 Holy Master, δεσποτης ο αγιος
37 x 45 mouth of God, (Matt. 4:4) στοματος Θεου
37 x 48 Lord of the sabbath, κυριοσ σαββατου

Science declares that numbers must occur at random unless there is intended design. The above demonstration of the use of the number 37 overwhelmingly points to intended design.

The intended design of the Creator is displayed in the heavens, it is displayed in the earth, it is displayed in nature, and in His written word. The study of gematria merely pulls back the curtain slightly, and allows a fleeting glimpse into the drama of the ages—the intended works of God. We see only pieces, but those tiny pieces tell us of a magnificent Creator!

Appendix II

The Rock Level Base of the Great Pyramid

The four corners of the Great Pyramid rest upon sockets that were sunk into the natural rock to an average depth of 9+ inches. The bedrock upon which this magnificent structure was built, rises beneath the interior of the Pyramid to the horizontal plane of the lower end of the floor of the first ascending passage. The base perimeter, however, rests on a platform placed upon this bedrock.

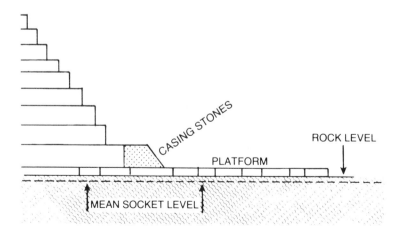

CASING STONES

ROCK LEVEL

PLATFORM

MEAN SOCKET LEVEL

The perimeter of the Great Pyramid at the level of its bedrock base is 3041 feet—a figure which does not seem at first to be of importance. However, upon further investigation, this rock base perimeter gives a startling confirmation of the correctness of other units of measure: the Great Cubit, the Reed[1], the Furlong, the British Mile, and the Megalithic Mile. This relationship is shown in the following table.

The Great Pyramid Rock Level Base—Full Design				
	1 Side	2 Sides	3 Sides	4 Sides
Feet	760.333	1520.666	2280.999	3041.333
Great Cubits	432.007	864.015	1296.002	1728.030
Reeds	72.001	144.002	216.003	288.005
Furlongs	1.152	2.304	3.456	4.608
British Miles	.144	.288	.432	.576
Megalithic Miles	.0528	.1056	.1584	.2112

As has been shown throughout the pages of this book, these are remarkable numbers indeed!

1 Side: 72 Reeds

   72   secret בסוד

   72   the truth, $\eta\ \alpha\lambda\eta\theta\epsilon\iota\alpha$

2 Sides: 144 Reeds

   144,000 = The number of those standing with the Lamb on Mount Zion (Rev. 14:1)

   144   the elect, $\eta\ \epsilon\kappa\lambda o\gamma\eta$

   1440 believers, $\pi\iota\sigma\tau\omega\nu$

   1440 elect of God, $\epsilon\kappa\lambda o\gamma\eta\nu\ \tau o\nu\ \Theta\epsilon o\nu$

   1440 purchased firstfruits, $\eta\gamma o\rho\alpha\sigma\theta\eta\sigma\alpha\nu\ \alpha\pi\alpha\rho\chi\eta$

---

1 The Great Cubit (1.76 feet) and the Reed (10.56 feet) were units of measure given to the prophet Ezekiel by God and recorded in Ezekiel 40:5 & 43:13.

ROCK LEVEL BASE

3 Sides: 216 Reeds
  216   power נְבוּרָה
  2160 Kingdom of the Father (Matt. 13:43),$\beta\alpha\sigma\iota\lambda\epsilon\iota\alpha$ $\tau\omega\nu$ $\pi\alpha\tau\rho\sigma\varsigma$
  2160 miles—diameter of the moon

4 Sides: 288 Reeds
  288   Kingdom of Heaven, (Matt. 13:47),$\beta\alpha\sigma\iota\lambda\epsilon\iota\alpha$ $\tau\omega\nu$ $\sigma\nu\rho\alpha\nu\omega\nu$
  2880 feet—diameter of Aubrey Circle at Stonehenge

1 Side: 432 Great Cubits
  432,000 miles—radius of sun
  432   a new name (Rev. 2:17), $o\nu o\mu\alpha$ $\kappa\alpha\iota\nu o\nu$
  432   all things (universe) (Rev. 21:5), $\pi\alpha\nu\tau\alpha$
  432   world (Psalm 96:13) תֵּבֵל
  432   habitation, $\kappa\alpha\tau\alpha\iota\kappa\iota\alpha$

2 Sides: 864 Great Cubits
  864,000 miles—diameter of sun
  864   flock of God, $\pi o\iota\mu\nu\iota o\nu$ $\Theta\epsilon o\upsilon$
  864   life, $\zeta\omega\eta\nu$
  864   the word of the Lord from Jerusalem (the New Jerusalem), (Micah 4:2), וּדְבַר יְהוָה מִירוּשָׁלָם
  864   God, $\Theta\epsilon\omega\nu$

3 Sides: 1296 Great Cubits
  1296 thou mayest be rich (Rev. 3:18), $\pi\lambda o\upsilon\tau\eta\sigma\eta\varsigma$

4 Sides: 1728 Great Cubits
  1728 the altar (Rev. 11:1), τo $\theta\upsilon\sigma\iota\alpha\sigma\tau\eta\rho\iota o\nu$
  1728 The God of my rock, he is my shield, and the horn of my salvation, my high tower and my refuge. (II Samuel 22:3), אלהי צורי מגני וקרן ישעי משגבי ומנוסי

APPENDIX II

1 Side: .144 Mile
    144,000—the number of those standing with the Lamb on
            Mount Zion, (Rev. 14:1)
    144   the elect, $\eta\ \varepsilon\kappa\lambda o\gamma\eta$
    1440 believers, $\pi\iota\sigma\tau\omega\nu$
    1440 elect of God, $\varepsilon\kappa\lambda o\gamma\eta\nu\ \tau o\upsilon\ \Theta\varepsilon o\upsilon$
    1440 purchased firstfruits, $\eta\gamma o\rho\alpha\sigma\theta\eta\sigma\alpha\nu\ \alpha\pi\alpha\rho\chi\eta$

2 Sides: .288 Mile
    288   Diameter of Aubrey Circle at Stonehenge
    2880 Kingdom of Heaven (Matt. 13:47), $\beta\alpha\sigma\iota\lambda\varepsilon\iota\alpha\ \tau\omega\nu$
    $o\upsilon\rho\alpha\nu\omega\nu$

3 Sides: .432 Mile
    432,000 miles—radius of sun
    432   a new name (Rev. 2:17), $o\nu o\mu\alpha\ \kappa\alpha\iota\nu o\nu$
    432   all things (universe), $\pi\alpha\nu\tau\alpha$
    432   world (Psalm 96:13)
    432   habitation, $\kappa\alpha\tau o\iota\kappa\iota\alpha$

4 Sides: .576 Mile
    576   thou art my Rock (Psa. 71:3,
    576   life (pneuma), $\pi\nu\varepsilon\upsilon\mu\alpha$
    576   in God is my salvation (Psa. 62:7),
            עַל־אֱלֹהִים יִשְׁעִי
    576   gospel, $\varepsilon\upsilon\alpha\gamma\gamma\varepsilon\lambda\iota o\nu$
    576   treasure, מִסְכְּנוֹת

1 Side: .0528 Megalithic Mile
    5280 feet in one British Mile
    528   royal, $\beta\alpha\sigma\iota\lambda\varepsilon\iota o\varsigma$
    528   shall be God's house (referring to the Bethel Stone),
            Gen. 28) יִהְיֶה בֵּית אֱלֹהִים

2 Sides: .1056 Megalithic Miles
    10.56 feet, length of each lintel in Sarsen Circle at Stonehenge.
    10,56 feet, length of the reed given as a measring rod to Ezekiel.
    1056   the joy of thy salvation (Psa. 51:12), שְׂשׂוֹן יִשְׁעֶךָ

3 Sides: .1584 Megalithic Mile
    1584   priests of God, ιερει του θεου
    1584   I will establish my covenant (Gen. 9:11),
         וַהֲקִמֹתִי אֶת־בְּרִיתִי
    1584   tabernacle (dwelling place) of God (Rev. 21:3), η κηνη του Θεου

4 Sides: .2112 Megalithic Miles
    2112   A virgin shall conceive and bear a son, and shall call his name Immanuel, (Isa. 7:14),
         הָעַלְמָה הָרָה וְיֹלֶדֶת בֵּן וְקָרָאת שְׁמוֹ עִמָּנוּ אֵל

The above corroboration of the numbers is too astounding to be mere coincidence! I believe it was the magnificent design of an intelligent Architect—an Architect who had an intimate knowledge of numbers, the language of the universe.

133

Appendix III

The Magic Square

Magic squares have been a fascinating toy for mathematicians for as long as there have been mathematicians.

The renowned Biblical scholar, E. W. Bullinger (*Number in Scripture*, 1894, page 286) recorded a magic square that I found to be truly exciting.

6	32	3	34	35	1
7	11	27	28	8	30
19	14	16	15	23	24
18	20	22	21	17	13
25	29	10	9	26	12
36	5	33	4	2	31

The square consists of 36 integers. The sum of the numbers 1 through 36 is 666. As has been shown, 666 is the number for *"head of the corner,"* describing the topstone of the Pyramid, but used symbolically to represent Jesus Christ. It is also the number for the imposter and counterfeit—the anti-christ.

Let's "play" with this magic square and discover its interesting qualities. As in all magic squares, the sum of each row, the sum of each column, and the sum of both diagonals, is the same number. In this case they each add up to 111.

The prophet Isaiah (9:6) told of the coming of the Messiah, and said *"His name shall be called Wonderful."* The Hebrew letters in that name have a number value of 111.

Thus we find that not only the total of all the numbers in this magic square refer to Jesus Christ, but the property that makes it "magic," the addition of the rows, columns, or diagonals, also refers to Him.

Magic squares usually stop with the addition of rows, columns and diagonals. This square, however, becomes more exciting the further we examine it.

The sum of all the numbers around the perimeter is 370. It is the gematria for the word "whole" as used in both Hebrew and Greek. The number 37 is a prime that is truly remarkable in its use in the titles of Jesus Christ. These are listed in Appendix I, pages 126 to 127.

This magic square, however, is dominated by the foundation number, 74. Each symetrical group of four numbers adds up to 74.

6	32	3	34	35	1
7	11	27	28	8	30
19	14	16	15	23	24
18	20	22	21	17	13
25	29	10	9	26	12
36	5	33	4	2	31

$(6 + 32 + 35 + 1 = 74)$

6	32	3	34	35	1
7	11	27	28	8	30
19	14	16	15	23	24
18	20	22	21	17	13
25	29	10	9	26	12
36	**5**	33	4	**2**	**31**

(36 + 5 + 2 + 31 = 74)

6	32	3	34	35	1
7	11	27	28	8	30
19	14	16	15	23	24
18	20	22	21	17	13
25	29	10	9	26	12
36	5	33	4	2	31

(6 + 7 + 25 + 36 = 74)

6	32	3	34	35	**1**
7	11	27	28	8	**30**
19	14	16	15	23	24
18	20	22	21	17	13
25	29	10	9	26	**12**
36	5	33	4	2	**31**

(1 + 30 + 12 + 31 = 74)

6	32	**3**	**34**	35	1
7	11	27	28	8	30
19	14	16	15	23	24
18	20	22	21	17	13
25	29	10	9	26	12
36	5	**33**	**4**	2	31

$$(3 + 34 + 33 + 4 = 74)$$

6	32	3	34	35	1
7	11	27	28	8	30
19	14	16	15	23	**24**
18	20	22	21	17	**13**
25	29	10	9	26	12
36	5	33	4	2	31

$$(19 + 18 + 24 + 13 = 74)$$

6	32	3	34	35	**1**
7	11	27	28	8	30
19	14	16	15	23	24
18	20	22	21	17	13
25	29	10	9	26	12
36	5	33	4	2	**31**

$$(6 + 1 + 36 + 31 = 74)$$

6	**32**	3	34	**35**	1
7	11	27	28	8	30
19	14	16	15	23	24
18	20	22	21	17	13
25	29	10	9	26	12
36	**5**	33	4	**2**	31

(32 + 35 + 5 + 2 = 74)

6	32	3	34	35	1
7	11	27	28	8	**30**
19	14	16	15	23	24
18	20	22	21	17	13
25	29	10	9	26	**12**
36	5	33	4	2	31

(7 + 30 + 25 + 12 = 74)

6	32	3	34	35	1
7	**11**	27	28	**8**	30
19	14	16	15	23	24
18	20	22	21	17	13
25	**29**	10	9	**26**	12
36	5	33	4	2	31

(11 + 8 + 29 + 26 = 74)

APPENDIX III

6	32	3	34	35	1
7	11	27	28	8	30
19	**14**	16	15	**23**	24
18	**20**	22	21	**17**	13
25	29	10	9	26	12
36	5	33	4	2	31

$(14 + 23 + 20 + 17 = 74)$

6	32	3	34	35	1
7	11	**27**	**28**	8	30
19	14	16	15	23	24
18	20	22	21	17	13
25	29	**10**	**9**	26	12
36	5	33	4	2	31

$(27 + 28 + 10 + 9 = 74)$

6	32	3	34	35	1
7	11	27	28	8	30
19	14	**16**	**15**	23	24
18	20	**22**	**21**	17	13
25	29	10	9	26	12
36	5	33	4	2	31

$(16 + 15 + 22 + 21 = 74)$

140

6	32	3	34	35	1
7	**11**	27	28	8	30
19	14	16	15	23	24
18	20	22	21	17	13
25	29	10	9	**26**	12
36	5	33	4	2	**31**

(6 + 11 + 26 + 31 = 74)

6	32	3	34	35	**1**
7	11	27	28	**8**	30
19	14	16	15	23	24
18	20	22	21	17	13
25	**29**	10	9	26	12
36	5	33	4	2	31

(1 + 8 + 29 + 36 = 74)

6	32	3	34	35	1
7	**11**	27	28	8	30
19	14	**16**	15	23	24
18	20	22	**21**	17	13
25	29	10	9	**26**	12
36	5	33	4	2	31

(11 + 16 + 21 + 26 = 74)

6	32	3	34	35	1
7	11	27	28	**8**	30
19	14	16	**15**	23	24
18	20	**22**	21	17	13
25	**29**	10	9	26	12
36	5	33	4	2	31

(8 + 15 + 22 + 29 = 74)

The number 74 dominates this magic square. I refer the reader to chapter 3, pages 43 through 47, which shows how the foundation number, 74, dominates the plan of God for the salvation of man through Jesus Christ.

If we were to eliminate the numbers in the perimeter, the total of the remainder of numbers would be 296.

6	32	3	34	35	1
7	11	27	28	8	30
19	14	16	15	23	24
18	20	22	21	17	13
25	29	10	9	26	12
36	5	33	4	2	31

296 has also been shown to represent salvation through Jesus Christ. Please refer to the list of gematria on page 44 for the exciting use of this number.

The number around the perimeter of this smaller square totals 222—a figure that has been shown to represent the inter-relationship of God and Jesus Christ. Please see list on page 15.

INDEX OF NUMBERS

Index of numbers, continued

144

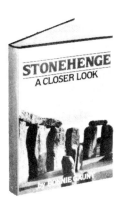